COLLEGE ENTRANCE

GAME PLAN

RYAN CLARK and DAN BISIG

College Entrance Game Plan
Your Comprehensive Guide to Collecting, Organizing, and Funding College
Ryan Clark and Dan Bisig

Copyright © 2016 by Ryan Clark and Dan Bisig
Published by:
Tuition Publishing
10130 Mallard Creek Rd
Suite 300
Charlotte, NC 28262

ISBN: 978-0-9831941-3-2

Library of Congress Control Number: 2016907515

First Edition, 2016

Published in the United States of America

For more information visit, www.clarkcollegefunding.com and www.collegeandbeyondllc.com

Dedication

This book is dedicated to my supportive and loving family, Rosie, Caden, and Carlene. It is also dedicated to all the families who want the most that college has to offer. Be bold, be courageous, be a leader, and be a friend.

Ryan Clark

I dedicate this book to my amazing wife Robin, awesome son Taylor, and incredible daughter Kendall. Without your love and support, this book would not have been possible. And to the terrific clients I have been lucky enough to work with over the years, THANK YOU for allowing me to be part of your fantastic journey, and here's to you reaching all of your future goals!

Dan Bisig

Disclaimer

This book is written to provide information and general guidance. The authors and publisher are not engaged in rendering legal, tax, or other professional advice. Refer to varying state and/or local laws, rules and/or regulations and engage the services of competent legal and tax professionals if assistance is needed or required.

It is not the purpose of this book to reprint all the information that is otherwise available to authors and/or publishers but instead to complement, amplify, and supplement other texts. Neither the authors nor the publisher assumes any responsibility for errors, omissions, or contradictory interpretation of the subject matter. You are urged to read all the available material about college planning and college financial aid and to tailor the information to your individual needs.

Although the information in the book has been proven effective, the reader or said purchaser assumes all responsibility for any and all usage. This text should be considered as a general guide, and every effort has been made to make this book as complete and as accurate as possible. However, there may be mistakes, both typographical and in content. You, said purchaser, reader, or user of this material, solely assume all responsibility for any and all such usage. Directly or indirectly, the authors and the publisher shall have neither liability nor responsibility to any person or entity with respect to any loss or damage caused by the information contained in this book. Moreover, the book contains information that is current only up to the printing date.

With this in mind, the author believes confidently that the information in this book may be used safely, legally, and successfully to educate and entertain readers on the simple steps to obtain *Affordable Solutions for the High Cost of Education*™. **If you do not wish to be bound by the above, you may return this book to the publisher for a full refund.**

Table of Contents

Acknowledgements

Thank you to the following individuals who, without their contributions and support, this book would not have been written.

To our incredible clients past, present and future who have inspired us to write this book. Thank you for allowing us to do what we love every day, help families navigate their way through every aspect of the college process!

To our friends in the HECA community who graciously edited chapters of this book with us: Suzann Cowing, Sandy Furth, Karen Scott Goldberg, Lisa Hillhouse, Chris Holzwarth, Cyndy McDonald, Heidi Price, Colleen Reed, Sheryl Santiago, Jennifer Sparrow, Jackie Stamps, Joan Thomas, and Judy Zodda.

To our friends in the NCAG community who helped edit chapters of this book with us: Fred Amrein, Gary Carpenter, and Al Hoffman.

To the many High Schools, PTSAs, Librarians, Churches, and Businesses who over the years have graciously invited us to share our College Workshops: Balluff Corp, Beechwood H.S., Bishop Brossart H.S., Boone County H.S., Boone County Public Library, Butler H.S., Cabarrus County Library Calvary Day School, Campbell County H.S., Clermont County Public Library, Concord H.S., Concord Library, Concord YMCA, Cooper H.S., Covenant Day, Covington Catholic H.S., Conner H.S., Covington Latin, Davidson Library, Dixie Heights H.S., East Forsyth H.S., Forest Hill Church, Fort Mill H.S., Gaston Christian, Gaston County Library, Greensboro Day, Hamilton County Library, Harrisburg Library, Harrisburg YMCA, Harvest Community Church, Highlands H.S., Huntington Learning Center Charlotte, Huntington Learning Center Huntersville, James Harris YMCA, Lake Norman H.S., Lake Norman YMCA, Matthews Library, Mint Hill Library, Mooresville Library, Morrison Library, Myers Park H.S., New Hanover County Library, Newport Central Catholic H.S., North County Library, North Mecklenburg H.S., Owen County H.S., Piedmont Community Charter, Ragsdale H.S., Reagan H.S., Ryle H.S., Salem Baptist Christian, Scott H.S., Simon Kenton H.S., South County Library, Southlake Christian, Steele Creek Library, The Palace, Toyota Motor Corporation, Villa Madonna, and Walton Verona H.S. Weddington H.S., West Cabarrus YMCA.

To our colleagues in the college planning world who have taught and inspired us to put everything we have learned through the years into this book: Tom and Lawrene Bottorf, Peter Van Buskirk, Rick Darvis, Mike Davila, Al Hoffman, Mark Kantrowitz, and Frank Palmasani.

To those who have contributed their expertise and/or help editing chapters of this book: Susan Knoppow and Kim Lift of *Wow Writing Workshop*, Lynn O'Shaughnessy of *The College Cost Lab*, Michelle Kretzschmar of *DIYcollegerankings*, Heather Luxon – veteran home educator, Chuck Moore of the *Educational Literacy Center*.

Finally, thank you to anyone and everyone whom we may have accidentally forgotten who had any part in helping us with our book. It takes a team!

WELCOME

Welcome to the *College Entrance Game Plan*! We congratulate you for investing in your future and entering the world of college planning and preparation. We are dedicated to your success and look forward to helping you navigate your way through what can at times seem like an intimidating process. In this incredible workbook (or organizational binder), you will learn powerful, time-tested principles and strategies that, if followed, can help you reach your personal goal of attending college and pay for it.

As you work through each of these chapters and tasks, you will be given the knowledge and tools you need to implement a successful and more stress-free college process.

Commitment

This workbook is designed to keep you organized and help you achieve the success you desire. However, if you are going to reach your goal, **YOU must decide to take action on a daily basis and stay committed to doing what only you can do: finishing strong!**

In this workbook, you will find a number of helpful tools to guide you through every step of the college planning process: starting as early as middle school and ending when you ultimately choose your final college. This workbook includes yearly timelines, valuable resources you will need, as well as checklists, worksheets, definitions, and dedicated chapters to help you keep organized and guide you every step of the way.

The Process

Receiving your college acceptance letters and getting an excellent financial aid package is a process. Like baking a cake, college planning requires many steps that must be followed in chronological order for it to turn out the way you planned. If not, you will be very disappointed with the results. Our goal with the "ideal timelines" in this book is to help you with these steps by clearly showing you what needs to be done in an organized and detailed fashion to help reduce your stress.

Team

These timelines were organized in a way for families to keep track of where they are in the college process. Many, if not all, of these steps, are meant to be completed as a family, not as individuals. It is important that you surround yourself with a solid team (parents, friends, teachers, counselors etc.).

Each school year, we encourage you to put the timelines in a location where the entire family can see them. This ensures that everyone is aware of the essential tasks that need to be completed each month and can help track where you are in the process.

Make it a point to put a "check mark" next to the steps as you complete them so you psychologically have a win, a small victory along the way. This will help keep you motivated to complete more tasks and stay on track.

If You Feel You Are Getting A Late Start, No Worries

If you are purchasing this workbook, and you think you are late in the college process, you simply need to change the months to weeks or maybe even days on the timelines. Depending on the amount of time and focus you give to the college process, your pace will vary compared to the given timelines. As you begin to work through your customized program, you will determine the pace that makes sense for you and your situation. We have also created the *Crucial College Checklist* to help you identify the essential college steps you need to complete.

Stay Organized

We created this workbook so you can stay organized. Every chapter builds on the next chapter to keep you on track and headed to your ultimate goal of getting accepted into your future college. **Take the time to get familiar with each section of your workbook.**

As you progress through our process and gather pertinent information, place it in the appropriate sections along the way. Keeping everything in one place will definitely make your college process easier.

To enhance your workbook, (depending upon which version of the *College Entrance Game Plan* you purchased) we encourage you to go to an office supply store and purchase:

- **A set of "31 Tab Index Dividers" (ex. Avery #11129), some page protectors, and plastic sleeves**
- **And pick up at least a 3", three ring binder** – you will need it!

Be prepared for an incredible amount of unsolicited college mail and emails students receive from a variety of colleges and universities through the years. Be strategic about what you do with this information, retaining only those schools that interest you and those you think you will apply to in the coming months. At the back of this organizer, we created a few dividers called **"College Booklets, Mail & Contacts"** (Chapters 28–31) to help you keep each of your school's literature separate. Please add more dividers as necessary for each of the colleges you decide to apply to in the future.

It is best to keep your workbook near where you open most of your college mail so that you can immediately deal with the volume of information as it comes in before it begins to take over your room. Yes, you will probably get that much mail! You will also notice we have created a page for you to keep up with your college logins. You will need this list when scheduling visits, applying, viewing your financial aid award packages, etc.

One Final Word of Advice

You will experience great success if you commit to approaching every step of this process positively and enthusiastically. There is a college out there that will meet your academic, financial, social, and geographical needs. Use this organizer daily to keep you on track so you can reach your college goal!

Wishing you all the best,
Ryan Clark and **Dan Bisig**

College Entrance Game Plan

College admissions is a complex, competitive, and complicated process. Moreover, the senior year in high school is often filled with many social activities, sporting events and academic requirements putting students on an emotional roller coaster filled with nervous anticipation of the coming school year. Because of this, even the most dedicated students and parents can feel overwhelmed and confused. To help reduce your stress level, you need to take action now and keep yourself organized using our family-tested filing, guidance and funding system.

Take Action

Our lives are often so busy that it is easy to get distracted and put things off, but when we are committed to something, we are more likely to take action toward it every day. For example, we are all determined to provide food and shelter for our family, so we take action and go to work every day to earn a paycheck to provide for our family. Without the commitment or the desire to support our family, we probably would not go to work every day. The same is true when it comes to jumping into the College Admissions Process.

We all want immediate results, but that is not how long term success is achieved. Success comes from working hard, following a proven plan, and taking action! In this book, we will show you how to organize your thoughts, systematize your plans, structure your paperwork, and map out your future. By following our process, success can be achieved. Now is the time to take action!

Organizational Binder

Staying organized throughout high school and especially during the senior year is critical so that you do not feel overwhelmed. Having a filing system where you can write your thoughts, keep track of deadlines, and systematize your paperwork is the key to staying focused and feeling in control. Not only will this binder reduce your stress during the last year of high school, but it will save you countless hours of lost time and frustration because you will have the necessary paperwork and information at your fingertips to complete many of the required college planning and application steps.

This binder has been set up in chronologically order to help you stay organized and focused from middle school through the very end of your high school career. Every academic year and month are mapped out for you making it easy to jump in no matter when you buy this binder or where you are in your academic life.

1. **Monthly Motivations**: College planning is achieved by following consecutive steps on a yearly basis. These sequential steps are predictable and organized with critical topics to help make your college planning process easier.

2. **7th Grade Organizational Timeline**: This is your monthly game plan for the 7th grade.

3. **8th Grade Organizational Timeline**: This is your monthly game plan for the 8th grade.

4. **9th Grade Organizational Timeline**: This is your monthly game plan for freshman year of high school.

5. **10th Grade Organizational Timeline:** This is your monthly game plan for sophomore year of high school.

6. **11th Grade Organizational Timeline:** This is your monthly game plan for your all important junior year of high school.

7. **12th Grade Organizational Timeline:** This is your monthly game plan for your critical senior year of high school.

8. **Annual Goals:** Here is a central location to have your annual goals recorded so you can focus your monthly efforts towards achieving them.

9. **Student Contact Information**: This information will be very handy when you call or speak to someone at a college. They will all ask for this information, so you need to have it in a convenient place for reference.

10. **Report Cards & Transcripts**: In this chapter you will keep a copy of your high school transcripts and report cards for future reference. Your report cards will allow you to check your transcript for any errors. (You might need to place your report cards in a page protector if you are not able to use a 3-hole punch).

11. **Career & College Major Search**: Students should complete a career search/personality assessment to identify their future career(s) and major before visiting colleges.

12. **Student Activity Records**: This chapter allows you to track your extracurricular activities and have information in one place to help with your future college applications. These activities include those you do in your high school or outside the school. Students with a range of outside-the-classroom experiences often do better in school, in the college admissions process, and in their adult lives.

13. **Awards & Recognitions**: This tab will help you keep your individual awards or special recognition safe during your high school career so they can be retrieved when completing lists of accomplishments on future college applications. (You might want to place each award into a separate clear page protector).

14. **AP / CLEP / DSST Exams**: If you decide to take AP courses, DSST tests, and/or CLEP exams in high school, you will need to keep track of the various tests you take and your scores. This tab will allow you to complete your college applications faster.

15. **Standardized Tests, Prep & Results**: Keeping your test results: PSAT, ACT, and SAT in one place will make it easy when it comes to completing future applications. Reviewing these results will help you identify subject areas you need to work on and determine the best test prep strategies and techniques to pursue.

16. **EFC Calculation**: Knowing your Expected Family Contribution (EFC) dollar amount number early will help you determine if your family will qualify for any need-based financial aid. Only then can you identify other college cost reducing strategies.

17. **College Budget**: When it comes to selecting a college, families need to determine how much college they can afford. This worksheet will help you speak honestly about the financial realities that most families face when it comes to paying for college. Make it a point to have this discussion as a family BEFORE final colleges are selected and applications are started.

18. **Paying for College**: Use this chapter to learn how to calculate your net cost and evaluate the various options to pay for college. By integrating and coordinating multiple strategies a successful college funding plan can be created and loans can be minimized.

19. **College Scholarship Search and Log**: Keeping track of the scholarships you are planning to apply for and tracking your scholarship deadlines is essential. Use this space to make sure you do not miss any important deadlines.

20. **College Visits & Evaluation**: Evaluate each college based on your selection criteria. Is it the right fit for you? After each visit, take time to jot down specific notes about each

college, 3-hole punch, and place them in your binder so you can refer back to your notes later.

21. **College Selection and Final College List**: Our suggestion is to do your research and ultimately apply to six colleges (2 Safety, 2 - 50/50 and 2 Reach) matching your academic, financial, social, and geographical FIT. This is a reasonable number of schools giving you a choice if you are not accepted by all of them. It also gives you a chance to compare financial aid packages offered by each school. Record the colleges and universities you plan to apply to in this section.

22. **College Resume & Letters of Recommendation**: While a resume may not be required (some high school counselors have their students just complete a brag sheet), a college resume can be very helpful when obtaining teacher recommendations, for college interviews, and to learn how to format and write a resume for the future.

23. **College, Scholarship and Honors Essays**: Keeping a hard copy of your college essay(s) is a smart thing to do. You never know when a computer disaster can ruin your day or when you can reallocate or slightly modify an existing essay for use with some other admissions or scholarship opportunity.

24. **College Applications & Financial Aid Form Deadlines**: Use this section to keep up with all the important deadlines for your college applications and financial aid forms. It is essential to stay organized.

25. **Student Aid Report (SAR)**: Print out and check the Student Aid Report (SAR) after completing the FAFSA form. You need to look for any errors on the SAR.

26. **Financial Aid Awards, Evaluations, & Appeal Letters**: If you complete the required financial aid forms and are accepted to a college, you will receive a financial aid package from each of your schools. Evaluate these financial aid awards to determine the net cost for each college so that you can make a good final decision. If you feel the amount of aid you have been offered at a college is inadequate, you can appeal your financial aid award. Learn more about this by reading the chapter.

27. **College Admission Terms & Resources**: Review and reference these important terms and definitions as you go through the college process. This Glossary will help.

28. **College Contacts / Booklets & Mail (Tabs 28-31)**: At the front of these dividers, you need to keep a list of names, phone numbers, e-mail addresses, etc. for individuals you may have met or might need to contact in the future at the colleges you are considering or in specific departments. Also within each divider, insert a page protector so you can

put any large or awkward booklets you receive. (Only keep information from the schools you are most interested in attending). Letters and other standard correspondence can be 3-hole punched and placed within the divider. You will also have a place to take notes in case you need to look back at them later. Add additional tabs if necessary.

The topics covered in this College Organizer will help you navigate your way through and have a successful college process. College research, coordinating college visits, making phone calls, gathering information on the financial aid process, completing financial aid forms, researching ways to evaluate awards, and writing appeal letters (if necessary) ALL require commitment, determination, and an enormous amount of time. **By starting now, success can be achieved!**

If you need assistance with any of these tasks, please contact us. We wish you the very best as you start this college planning process and work toward accomplishing your dreams!

Remember to visit Coach Dan's website www.collegeandbeyondllc.com and Coach Ryan's website www.collegeaidformiddleclass.com

Crucial College Checklist

This Checklist represents what we feel are the *minimum steps* you should complete for your college planning process. It was created to help all families, but especially those who feel they are behind schedule or those who want the basic requirements to have a successful college planning experience.

This organizer was designed for parents and students to systematize the college process so you can stay on track. We have created the individual Grade Level Ideal Timelines and the individual chapters to give you a specific monthly "To Do List", where each step is expanded upon in detail.

☐ **1. Use Your College Entrance Game Plan Binder**

This binder is a critical tool to keep you on track and will be an indispensable resource for you.

☐ **2. Complete a Career Assessment**

Understanding who you are is important. A Career Assessment can help identify your strengths and weaknesses based on your current interests, skills, values and personality.

☐ **3. Select A Major**

Using the personality assessment results, you can choose a future career and a corresponding major you would like to study in college. You can also see if the career or major you were already considering matches who you are.

☐ **4. Clean Up Your Social Media Profiles**

Many colleges are checking your profiles, pictures, posts, and doing research on you. Please make sure you are representing yourself in the best possible way.

☐ **5. Register and Take the SAT/ACT**

Deadlines to register can come up quickly, so register well in advance. To view testing dates and registration deadlines, visit www.collegeboard.org for the SAT and www.act.org for the ACT.

☐ **6. Study and Prepare to Take the SAT/ACT/PSAT Test**

When possible use a book, tutor, online prep program, or group test prep program to help you prepare for and maximize your score.

☐ **7. Calculate Your Expected Family Contribution (EFC) Number**

Knowing your EFC number will help you determine what financial aid options will be offered to you. Visit http://www.collegeboard.org and search for "EFC Calculator" to run your number.

☐ **8. Create A College Budget**

It is important to have a family discussion on affordability and fit BEFORE you apply to any colleges. Knowing your EFC number will help you understand what the colleges are going to expect so you can implement effective strategies to reduce the cost of the college you chose.

☐ **9. Create A College List**

Put together a list of schools you feel would be a good fit for you: academically, financially, socially and geographically.

☐ **10. Visit Colleges**

The best way to find out if a college is a good social fit for you is to schedule an official visit, walk around the campus and learn more about the school. These visits will help you verify how you feel after visiting and give you a better sense of what college life will be like on each campus.

☐ **11. Know Your College Application and Financial Aid Requirements and Deadlines**

Admission requirements and deadline dates vary drastically from school to school. Decide if you will be submitting a Regular Decision, Early Decision, or Early Action application. You need to keep track of these requirements and deadlines because you DO NOT want to miss these critical dates. Many colleges will list their application deadlines on their websites during the summer and also any additional application requirements.

☐ **12. Apply to Colleges**

Start applying to colleges in late summer to late fall of your senior year in high school. Early Action and Early Decision deadlines can occur as early as October 1st.

☐ **13. Complete & Submit Financial Aid Forms**

Families need to complete the Free Application for Federal Student Aid (FAFSA), and when necessary the CSS Profile or Financial Aid Profile (FAP), and/or required institutional forms. These forms go live October 1st but check each college to confirm their submission deadlines. Some colleges will also request additional forms to be completed.

☐ 14. Review Your Financial Aid Award Letters

You need to determine how much it will cost to attend each college before making a final college selection. Official financial aid Award Letters usually arrive in the spring (Feb-April) of the senior year of high school. This is also when you can appeal your award if necessary.

☐ 15. May 1st – National Decision Day

Compare the awards you received to your budget before **May 1st** so your family can make a good college selection. After you have made your decision, please inform the chosen college and send in your enrollment deposit by May 1st. It is also appropriate for you to let any other colleges you were accepted too know that you will not be attending their college.

☐ 16. Schedule your Freshman Orientation Date

The earlier you get your freshman orientation date scheduled the better. You do not want to discover when you go to orientation that the only classes still open are General Ed Classes. **Do not procrastinate!**

☐ 17. Review Payment and Loan Options

There are many ways to pay for college and it is important to consider all your options **BEFORE** you take out a loan. For federal student loans, you will need to complete the paperwork at www.studentloans.gov. Also consider private educational loans ONLY as a last resort option. Make sure all loan applications are complete and the funds are distributed to your college.

Here is to your College Success!

Remember to visit Coach Dan's website www.collegeandbeyondllc.com and Coach Ryan's website www.collegeaidformiddleclass.com

"You have to have an enthusiasm for life. You have to have a dream, a goal. And you have to be willing to work for it."

- Jimmy Valvano, Coach

Proper College Planning is achieved by following chronological steps on a yearly basis. You will find that the monthly topics on the yearly timelines are the same from year to year. For example, the topic of "Exploring Who You Are" is the theme for the month of August in seventh grade as well as eighth through twelfth grade. These monthly "to do lists" are organized to make college planning easy and predictable. We call this your "Monthly Motivations." You will notice that the individual task may change from year to year as you get closer to high school graduation, but the theme of the Monthly Motivations remains the same. Below are the descriptions and theme for each of the Monthly Motivations on your timeline:

August: Exploring Who You Are

"To be successful you must first decide exactly what you want to accomplish, then resolve to pay the price to get it." – Bunker Hunt

In life, we are often on a quest to figure out who we are and what our future purpose is going to be. Students often ask themselves: What do I want to do for the rest of my life?

The good news is there are some great resources and analysis programs available to help you search for your future calling. In each tab of this college organizer, we have listed some of our favorite resources to assist you. Each year we will be asking you to complete tasks to help explore who you are, what you enjoy doing, and what career opportunities you may want to pursue in the future. Identifying what makes you unique and discovering your future college major is important which is why you will spend time every August exploring who you are!

September: Designing Your Future

"I will prepare and some day my chance will come." – Abraham Lincoln

During this month, we will explore ways to help you identify your goals and provide you with some great tools you can use to achieve them. We want you to DREAM about what your future looks like and have a plan to achieve your dreams. September's theme is helping you plan your future.

October: College Preparation

"Spectacular achievement is always preceded by spectacular preparation."   - Robert H. Schuller

When it comes to positioning yourself for college, everything begins with a solid foundation and proper preparation. Over the next few days, weeks, months and years (depending upon when you start this organizer) you will find the exact steps needed to prepare you for college. During the month of October, we will focus on what it takes to position you as a viable candidate for the colleges you are considering applying to.

November: Becoming a Balanced Student

"Truly successful decision making relies on a balance between deliberate and instinctive thinking." - Malcolm Gladwell

Colleges like to see a broad range of talents in their incoming freshman class. However, not all colleges are looking for the same type of student or talents. Some schools might be looking for the "best of the best" while others may be looking for the most unusual talents or perspectives.

In an attempt to build up their applications and resume with tons of involvement, some students will bounce around when it comes to membership in clubs, jobs, sports, and other activities. However, College Admission Officers are looking to see if you have shown dedication to a cause by demonstrating substantive involvement, achieving a goal, and showing leadership. Better to be dedicated to a few activities than to be over committed to way too many.

November's Monthly Motivation will help you focus on becoming a well rounded and balanced student.

December: Capitalize on Your Time Off

"Free time is a terrible thing to waste. Read a book." — E.A. Bucchianeri

The month of December is a wonderful time to celebrate the holidays and appreciate spending time with your family and friends. It is also a great time to read a book for pleasure or get involved in organizations and events around your community where you can make a positive impact. Don't be afraid to try something new or do something that is out of your comfort zone. Some of your best life experiences and memories might come from these special times.

1

In many cases, you will find you have a break from school work during this month. Let's take advantage of this time off so you can further your college goals. December's Monthly Motivation will focus on small, but simple tasks that will save you time and make a big impact later in the year.

January: Money Matters

"Money is better than poverty, if only for financial reasons."   - Woody Allen

As the New Year starts, it is a great time to reflect on the past year and set your New Year's resolution. It is also time for you to learn about college financial aid, become financially literate, and implement strategies to reduce the cost of college.

The truth is, we all must know how money works especially when it comes to paying for college. One of the MOST IMPORTANT conversations parents and students must have is: HOW ARE YOU GOING TO PAY FOR COLLEGE?

The January's Monthly Motivation topic is all about money. College is an expensive investment, and we know your money matters. We will be giving you tasks and tools to help you become an informed college consumer and help educate you on college financial literacy terms.

February: Monitor Your Direction

"If we don't change direction soon, we'll end up where we're going."   - Professor Irwin Corey

It's time to take ownership of your future and take command of where you are heading. By seeking out information, you can clearly see where you are today. Are you making good decisions? Do you need to make a change for the better? Are you trending up or down?

You will spend time in February observing the direction you are heading and make necessary corrections to keep you on course. The route to owning your future starts with monitoring your direction.

March: Academic & Curriculum Strategy

"Knowledge without know-how is sterile. We use the word 'academic' in a pejorative sense to identify this limitation." - Myron Tribus

Your academic and curriculum strategy is an essential component to college planning success. Some courses better prepare students for postsecondary-level work than any other factor. The U.S. Department of Education in the publication "Answers In The Tool Box" published on 6/1/1999 found a strong correlation between high school curriculum and obtaining a bachelor's degree:

"The high school curriculum reflects 41% of the academic resources students bring to higher education; test scores, 30%; and class rank/academic GPA, 29%. No matter how one divides the universe of students, the curriculum measure produces a higher percent earning bachelor's degrees than either of the other two measures. The correlation of curriculum with bachelor's degree attainment is also higher (.54) than test scores (.48) or class rank/GPA (.44)."

Mapping out your Academic Plan can be a huge challenge. We will guide you through this process and give you homework to complete to help you stay on target with your academic and curriculum strategy.

March's Monthly Motivation will focus on tracking and mapping out your Academic & Curriculum Strategy. It is essential that you take the time to choose the right classes needed to reach your college and career goals.

April: Research and Preparation

"There are no secrets to success. It is the result of preparation, hard work, and learning from failure." - Colin Powell

Spring is the time for rebirth, research, and preparation. Whether it is preparing for the Standardized Tests, or planning your college visits, the month of April is dedicated to these undertakings.

Taking some form of standardized test is an ever present part of going to college. Even when you get to College, and depending upon what Career aspirations you have, it is possible you will be forced to take additional tests (GRE, MCAT, JD etc.) in order to pursue your future career.

We believe you should educate yourself about the significance of every test and identify the best ways to prepare for them. Better to start early than to scramble and stress at the end.

May: Adapt and Adjust

"Adapt or perish, now as ever, is nature's inexorable imperative." - H. G. Wells

Change is inevitable! A student's grades may slip because they bomb a quiz or test, maybe their family moves, favorite teachers retire, parents lose jobs, family members become sick, students get placed in classes with teachers they do not like, etc. During these crucial years of your life, you may go through a roller coaster of emotions because of the dramatic changes you will be encountering.

May is also the time of year when you prepare to change grade levels or move on to college. With this change, you will need tools and strategies to help make this transition easier.

This month's Monthly Motivation will focus on helping you quickly cope with the ever present change in your life.

Summer: All About Autumn

"September tries its best to have us forget summer." - Bern Williams

Starting off the new school year with the right focus and mindset can lead to a rewarding and successful school year and a successful August depends on what you accomplished in the months of June and July!

For many of us, summer is the time for family vacations and rejuvenation. But it can also be a wonderful time to use some of your free time to prepare for the upcoming school year.

All About Autumn is the Monthly Motivation for the months of June and July. We will share some of the best summer activities you can do to help prepare you for the beginning of school.

Parting Thoughts:

Regardless of your grade level, it is important for you to remember that you are captaining your ship. You are in charge of setting sail each year and deciding where you are headed. Will you run into obstacles throughout the school year? It is a strong possibility; but if you surround yourself with a team of individuals who care about you and will help you navigate your way around these challenges, success can be achieved!

It is important from day one to remember that you start each new school year with a clean slate. Every day you have to make a CHOICE. Are you going to make the necessary sacrifices to achieve your goals or are you going to pay the price by your inactivity? Remember, to be successful in the college process, *you must be proactive about following the timelines and completing each task!*

Start strong, choose to be focused, and do everything possible to reach your goals!

7th Grade Organizational Timeline

"You can motivate by fear, and you can motivate by reward. But both those methods are only temporary. The only lasting thing is self-motivation."

— Homer Rice, Football Player & Coach

August Exploring Who You Are

☐ Complete a Career/Interest Inventory to see how your interests relate to the Working World (Chapter 11).

☐ Practice writing a college essay on what you want your life to be like after high school (put in Chapter 23).

☐ Research career interests (Chapter 11).

☐ Make a list of any school clubs, civic organizations, religious service groups, and community service projects you might like to join (Chapter 12.

September Designing Your Future

☐ Express to your family that you would like to go to college and talk about your goals together.

☐ Research recent high school graduates who received college scholarships and write down their accomplishments.

☐ Write down your goals for the year: academic, athletic, work, extra-curricular, etc. (Chapter 8).

October College Preparation

☐ Look for projects and activities that allow you to develop time-management, communication, and leadership skills.

☐ Research your local high school and determine what advance course opportunities you will have available and what you need to do in middle school to be ready IF you choose to pursue them.

☐ Pay particular attention to courses that help you learn Science, Technology, Engineering, and Math (STEM) and/or Art (STEAM).

November Becoming a Balanced Student

☐ Start to build your resume by using your leadership skills in various projects (place in Chapter 22).

☐ Start or become a member of a school club, civic organization, religious service group, or join a community service project.

☐ Start a business or non-profit organization.

☐ Plan on playing a sport in the spring.

☐ Explore possible careers and make new friends.

☐ Make it a point to read something new every day. Reading and problem solving are both important skills to master for your future.

December — Capitalize on Your Time Off

2

- ☐ Reach out to friends/relatives who are already in college and get their advice about preparing and planning for college.

- ☐ Look for ways to assist in a school, religious or community service project during the holiday break.

- ☐ Talk to an adult you admire about their career path.

- ☐ Go to a few college websites. Watch available virtual college tours and record (in Chapter 20) any schools you might be interested in.

January — Money Matters

- ☐ Look for local college and career fairs that you can attend in the coming months.

- ☐ Start researching your local high school options and gather information to help with a smooth transition into high school.

- ☐ Find out if you can gain high school credit in 8th grade.

- ☐ Review your yearly goals to see if you are on track to meet them. Do you need to adjust your behavior or attitude to reach the goals you set for yourself? Do you need to make new habits or follow a new path? Are you making good decisions about your future (Chapter 8)?

February   Monitor Your Direction

☐ Look for ways to assist in a school, religious or community service project during the holiday break.

☐ Talk to an adult you admire about their career path.

☐ Go to a few college websites. Watch available virtual college tours and record (in Chapter 20) any schools you might be interested in visiting.

March   Academic & Curriculum Strategy

☐ Learn about college credit you can earn while in high school: AP, IB, CLEP, Community College, Dual Enrollment, Early College, etc. (Chapter 14).

☐ Research all your class options for the 8th grade.

☐ Plan your electives for 8th grade.

April   Research and Preparation

☐ Do your best on your end-of-year or course tests.

☐ Review your goals on class rank, GPA (grade point average) and course selection. Do you need help with a subject (Chapter 8)?

☐ Take advantage of mentors, tutors, and extra study sessions.

| *May* | Adapt and Adjust | 2 |

- ☐ Consider attending summer camps or programs that will help you get ahead in school.

- ☐ Look for registration deadlines for summer programs at school or local colleges.

- ☐ Continue to research and join a local service project that needs volunteers (Chapter 12).

| *Summer* | All About Autumn |

- ☐ Attend summer camps or activities that will help you grow as a person, find new friends, or learn something new.

- ☐ Stay active during the summer: physically and mentally.

- ☐ Review your monthly budget to see how you are doing (Chapter 17).

- ☐ Find a way to earn extra money: a part-time job, start a business, or identify ways to increase your allowance.

- ☐ Go to 8th grade orientation.

- ☐ Work on a local community service project. Focus on helping others and improving your leadership skills (Chapter 12)

8th Grade Organizational Timeline

"It's not whether you get knocked down; it's whether you get up."

– Vince Lombardi, Player & Coach

3

August — Exploring Who You Are

☐ Complete a learning-style assessment survey to gain a better understanding of yourself and determine your own personal learning style.

☐ Practice writing a college essay on what you would like to accomplish during the 8th grade.

☐ Continue to research career interests (Chapter 11) and look for ways to job shadow any careers that interest you.

☐ Add to your activity record (Chapter 12) any school clubs, civic organizations, religious service groups, and service projects you completed this past year.

September — Designing Your Future

☐ Write down your goals for the year: academic, athletic, work, extra-curricular, etc.

☐ Express to your family that you would like to be a college graduate and together talk about your goals.

☐ Discuss with your parents careers that might interest you and see if they have any friends or relatives in that field with whom you can speak about their career (Chapter 11).

October College Preparation

☐ Research recent high school graduates who received college scholarships and write down the activities and accomplishments in which they were involved (Chapter 19).

☐ Make specific plans to join projects/activities that allow you to develop time-management, communication, and leadership skills.

☐ Research your local high school and determine what advance course opportunities you will have available to you during 9th grade IF you choose to pursue them.

☐ Pay particular attention to courses that help you learn Science, Technology, Engineering, and Math (STEM) and/or Art (STEAM).

November Becoming a Balanced Student

☐ Look for ways to be involved in a sport or other extra-curricular activities.

☐ Find ways to build your resume by using your leadership skills in various projects (Chapter 12).

☐ Start or become a member of a school club, civic organization, religious service group, or join a community service project.

☐ Consider starting a business or non-profit organization.

☐ Use all of these opportunities to explore possible careers, build your resume, and make new friends (Chapter 22).

December — Capitalize on Your Time Off

☐ Look for opportunities to speak with friends/relatives about their college experiences.

☐ Look for ways to assist in a school, religious or community service project during the holiday break.

☐ Talk to an adult you admire about their career path.

☐ Visit a few local college websites. Schedule visits with your parents in the spring when you will be able to have an informal visit to see how different colleges look and feel (Chapter 20).

3

January — Money Matters

☐ Know the basics about financial aid for college: loans, work study, scholarships, and grants (Chapter 24).

☐ Plan a budget for the next few months (Chapter 17).

☐ Discuss with an adult the difference between a need versus a want.

February   Monitor Your Direction

☐ Look for local college and career fairs you can attend in the coming months.

☐ Review your yearly goals to see if you are on track to meet them. Do you need to adjust your behavior or attitude to reach the goals you set for yourself? Do you need to make new habits or follow a new path? Are you making good decisions about your future (Chapter 8)?

☐ Start researching local high school options and gather information to help you transition into high school.

☐ Complete a four-year plan. Some middle schools host events to help eighth graders plan the next four years of high school. If your school does not, then schedule a meeting with a guidance counselor and parent to discuss your future options for high school.

March   Academic & Curriculum Strategy

☐ Learn about college credit you can earn while in high school: AP, IB, CLEP, Community College, Dual Enrollment, Early College, etc. (Chapter 14).

☐ Research all your class options for the 9th grade.

☐ Plan your electives for 9th grade.

☐ Know that GPA is the first thing colleges look at and consider during the admissions process. Make it a yearly goal to work hard on your GPA, class rank, and course selection (Chapter 10).

April	Research and Preparation

3

☐ Do your best on your end-of-year or course tests.

☐ Review your goals on class rank, GPA (grade point average) and course selection.

☐ Be honest with yourself in subjects that are giving you trouble.

☐ If needed, ask for assistance from teachers, mentors, tutors, and do extra study sessions.

May	Adapt and Adjust

☐ Consider attending summer camps or programs that will help you get ahead in school or expand your mind.

☐ Look for registration deadlines for summer programs at school or local colleges.

☐ Continue to research and join a local service project that needs volunteers (Chapter 12).

Summer	All About Autumn

☐ Go to 9th grade orientation, tour your high school, meet your teachers, and find your classroom.

☐ Attend summer camps or activities that will help you grow as a person, find new friends, or learn something new.

☐ Stay active during the summer: physically and mentally.

☐ Review your monthly budget to see how you are doing (Chapter 17).

☐ Find a way to earn extra money: a part-time job, start a small business, or identify ways to increase your allowance.

☐ Work on a local community service project. Focus on helping others and improving your leadership skills (Chapter 12).

9th Grade Organizational Timeline

"The only place that success comes before work is in the dictionary."

– Vince Lombardi, Player & Coach

August	Exploring Who You Are

☐ Complete a learning-style assessment survey to gain a better understanding of yourself and determine your own personal learning style.

☐ Practice writing a college essay using the Common Application essay prompts (put in Chapter 23).

☐ Continue to research career interests (Chapter 11) and look for ways to set up job-shadowing opportunities in careers that interest you.

☐ Review College Resume & Letters of Recommendation section and start your Student Resume (Chapter 22).

☐ Start off the school year strong. Know that GPA is the first thing that all colleges look at and consider.

☐ Ask your Counselor if your high school recalculates your Composite GPA in your senior year at the end of a quarter or fall semester OR if they will only submit your junior year ending composite GPA to all of your colleges.

September — Designing Your Future

☐ Write down your goals for the year: academic, athletic, work, extra-curricular, etc. (Chapter 8).

☐ Express to your family that you would like to be a college graduate and together talk about your goals.

☐ Discuss with your parents careers that might interest you and see if they have any friends or relatives in that field with whom you can speak about their career (Chapter 11).

☐ Make specific plans to join projects/activities that allow you to develop time-management, communication, and leadership skills.

October — College Preparation

☐ Try to start visiting many different types of colleges to get a feel for what is available to you: large, small, public, and private (Chapter 20).

☐ Write down colleges that pique your interest and why you find them appealing (Chapter 21).

☐ Research the various paths to earning a post-secondary degree and entrance requirements for each option (e.g., community college, junior college, technical college, online college).

November   Becoming a Balanced Student

4

☐ Look for ways to be involved in a sport or other extra-curricular activities.

☐ Build your student resume by joining a service project and improving your leadership skills (Chapter 22).

☐ Make plans to start a business or non-profit organization.

☐ Explore possible careers and make new friends (Chapter 11).

☐ Make it a point to read something new every day. Reading and problem solving are both essential skills to master for your future.

December   Capitalize on Your Time Off

☐ Become familiar with any words or terms associated with college admissions with which you might not be familiar (Chapter 27).

☐ Look for opportunities to speak with friends/relatives about their college experiences.

☐ Look for ways to assist in a school, religious or community service project during the holiday break.

☐ Talk to adults you admire about their college and career paths.

☐ Continue to schedule your college visits for the rest of the year (Chapter 20).

☐ Check your GPA and make sure you are on target.

January Money Matters

☐ Know the definitions and the differences between loans, work study, scholarships, tuition discounts, and grants (Chapter 25 and 27).

☐ Plan a budget for the next few months (Chapter 17).

☐ Discuss with an adult the difference between a private scholarship vs. a college specific scholarship (Chapter 19).

☐ Research recent high school graduates who received college scholarships and write down all the activities and accomplishments in which they were involved (Chapter 19).

☐ Know the definition of Expected Family Contribution (EFC) and the impact this dollar amount plays in the type and amount of financial aid you and your family will receive (Chapter 16).

☐ Discuss with your parents how much your family can afford to put toward your college education on an annual basis. Remember, college can run as much as $16,000 per year for an in-state public university to more than $65,000 per year for a private college.

☐ Have you run your EFC (Expected Family Contribution)? If there is any chance (based on your family's Adjusted Gross Income AND the colleges you are applying to) that you might qualify for some need based financial aid, now is the time to consider what to do with custodial accounts and the impact them might have on the type of aid you receive. Contact a qualified financial advisor, college planner, or CPA to explore your options today.

February — Monitor Your Direction

☐ Look for local college and career fairs you can attend in the coming months.

☐ Review your yearly goals to see if you are on track to meet them. Do you need to adjust your behavior or attitude to reach the goals you set for yourself? Do you need to make new habits or follow a new path? Are you making good decisions about your future (Chapter 8)?

☐ Create an email account that you can use for communicating with colleges.

☐ Pay particular attention to your online accounts and clean up your image if necessary.

4

March — Academic & Curriculum Strategy

☐ Learn about college credit you can earn while in high school: AP, IB, CLEP, Community College, Dual Enrollment, Early College, etc. (Chapter 14).

☐ Make sure you are taking the required courses needed for college admissions. Remember, these requirements and expectations can be different the more competitive the college.

☐ Plan your electives for 10th grade.

☐ Make it a yearly goal to work hard on your GPA, class rank, and course selection (Chapter 8).

April   Research and Preparation

☐ Do your best on your end-of-year or course tests.

☐ Find out about the PSAT/NMSQT, ASPIRE (Chapter 14) pre-college admission tests and what will be offered at your high school.

☐ Be honest with yourself on how you are doing in your subjects.

☐ If needed, ask for assistance from teachers, mentors, tutors, and extra study sessions.

☐ Plan ahead for AP/IB exams by finding out more about the tests.

May   Adapt and Adjust

☐ Update your college resume (Chapter 22) on the items you have accomplished this year.

☐ Consider attending summer camps or programs that will help you get ahead in school or expand your mind.

☐ Look for registration deadlines for summer programs at school or local colleges.

☐ Continue to research and join a local service project that needs volunteers (Chapter 12).

Summer	All About Autumn	**4**

☐ Review your yearly goals to see how you did (Chapter 8).

☐ Decide what you would like to accomplish or achieve over the summer and make plans.

☐ Attend summer camps or activities that will help you grow as a person, find new friends, or learn something new.

☐ Stay active during the summer: physically and mentally.

☐ Review your monthly budget to see how you are doing (Chapter 17).

☐ Find a way to earn extra money, find a part-time job, start a small business, identify ways to increase your allowance, etc.

☐ Work on a local community service project. Focus on helping others and improving your leadership skills (Chapter 12).

☐ Visit more colleges or universities (Chapter 20).

10th Grade Organizational Timeline

"Perfection is not attainable, but if we chase perfection we can catch excellence."

– Vince Lombardi, Player & Coach

August	Exploring Who You Are

5

☐ Complete a learning-style assessment survey to gain a better understanding of yourself and determine your own personal learning style.

☐ Practice writing a college essay using the Common Application essay prompts (put in Chapter 23).

☐ Continue to research career interests (Chapter 11) and look for ways to set up job-shadowing opportunities in careers that interest you.

☐ Review College Resume & Letters of Recommendation section and start your Student Resume (Chapter 22).

☐ Start off the school year strong. Know that GPA is the first thing that all colleges look at and consider.

September — Designing Your Future

☐ Write down your goals for the year: academic, athletic, work, extra-curricular, etc. (Chapter 8).

☐ Express to your family that you would like to be a college graduate and together talk about your goals.

☐ Discuss with your parents careers that might interest you and see if they have any friends or relatives in that field with whom you can speak about their career (Chapter 11).

☐ Make specific plans to join projects/activities that allow you to develop time-management, communication, and leadership skills.

☐ Do your research on taking the PSAT or Pre-ACT Exams

October — College Preparation

☐ Try to start visiting many different types of colleges to get a feel for what is available to you: large, small, public, and private (Chapter 20).

☐ Write down colleges that pique your interest and why you find them appealing (Chapter 21).

☐ Research the various paths to earning a post-secondary degree and entrance requirements for each option (e.g., community college, junior college, technical college, online college).

November   Becoming a Balanced Student

☐ Look for ways to be involved in a sport or other extra-curricular activities in the winter and spring months.

☐ Build your student resume by joining a service project and improving your leadership skills (Chapter 22).

☐ Make plans to start a business or non-profit organization.

☐ Explore possible careers and make new friends (Chapter 22).

☐ Make it a point to read something new every day.

☐ Reading and problem solving are essential skills to master for your future.

5

December   Capitalize on Your Time Off

☐ Become familiar with any words or terms associated with college admissions with which you might not be familiar (Chapter 27).

☐ Look for opportunities to speak with friends/relatives about their college experiences.

☐ Look for ways to assist in a school, religious or community service project during the holiday break.

☐ Talk to adults you admire about their college and career paths.

☐ Continue to schedule your college visits for the rest of the year (Chapter 20).

☐ Check your GPA and make sure you are on target.

January   Money Matters

☐ Know the definitions and the differences between loans, work study, scholarships, tuition discounts, and grants (Chapter 25 and 27).

☐ Plan a budget for the next few months (Chapter 17).

☐ Discuss with an adult and understand the difference between a private scholarship vs. a college specific scholarship (Chapter 19).

☐ Research who received college scholarships from your high school and write down their accomplishments and all the activities in which they were involved (Chapter 19). Try to identify what made them stand out?

☐ Know the definition of Expected Family Contribution (EFC) and the impact this dollar amount plays in the type and amount of financial aid you and your family will receive (Chapter 16).

☐ If you have not already done so, talk with your parents about how much they can afford to put toward helping pay for your college education on an annual or monthly basis. Remember, college can run as much as $16,000 per year for an in-state public university to more than $65,000 per year for a private college.

☐ Attend a college fair to get more information and learn more about your future colleges. NACAC (and many high schools) sponsor college fairs in cities across the country during the fall and spring. To learn more about the NACAC fairs, visit www.nationalcollegefairs.org for dates and locations.

February — Monitor Your Direction

☐ Review your yearly goals to see if you are on track to meet them. Do you need to adjust your behavior or attitude to reach the goals you set for yourself? Do you need to make new habits or follow a new path? Are you making good decisions about your future (Chapter 8)?

☐ Create an email account that you can use for communicating with colleges and submitting private college scholarship applications.

☐ Pay particular attention to your online accounts and clean up your image if necessary.

5

March — Academic & Curriculum Strategy

☐ Schedule a time to meet with your guidance counselor to help you decide on options for advanced or honors courses next year.

☐ Learn about college credit you can earn while in high school: AP, IB, CLEP, Community College, Dual Enrollment, Early College, etc. (Chapter 14).

☐ Make sure you are taking the required courses needed for college admissions. Remember, these requirements and expectations can be different the more competitive the college.

☐ Plan your electives for 11th grade.

☐ Make it a yearly goal to work hard on your GPA, class rank, and course selection (Chapter 8).

April — Research and Preparation

☐ Do your best on your end-of-year or course tests.

☐ Be honest with yourself on how you are doing in your subjects.

☐ If needed, ask for assistance from teachers, mentors, tutors, and schedule extra study sessions.

☐ Plan ahead for AP/IB exams by finding out more about the tests.

May — Adapt and Adjust

☐ Update your college resume (Chapter 22) on the items you have accomplished this year.

☐ Consider attending summer camps or programs that will help you get ahead in school or expand your mind.

☐ Look for registration deadlines for summer programs at school or local colleges.

☐ Continue to research and join a local service project that needs volunteers (Chapter 12).

Summer	All About Autumn

5

☐ Review your yearly goals to see how you did (Chapter 8).

☐ Decide what you would like to accomplish or achieve over the summer and make plans.

☐ Attend summer camps or activities that will help you grow as a person, find new friends, or learn something new.

☐ Stay active during the summer: physically and mentally.

☐ Review your monthly budget to see how you are doing (Chapter 17).

☐ Find a way to earn extra money: find a part-time job, start a small business, identify ways to increase your allowance. Be creative!

☐ Work on a local community service project. Focus on helping others and improving your leadership skills (Chapter 12).

☐ Visit more colleges or universities (Chapter 20).

11th Grade Organizational Timeline

"The key is not the will to win. Everybody has that. It is the will to prepare to win that is important."

— Bobby Knight, Coach

August	Exploring Who You Are

☐ If you have not already completed a career analysis program (see Chapter 11) do it now so that you can find options that match you.

☐ Find careers that you will excel in and enjoy.

☐ Select a college major (Chapter 11) that will prepare you for your future career path.

☐ Practice writing a college essay using the Common Application essay prompts (put in Chapter 23).

☐ Review the College Resume & Letters of Recommendation section and update your Student Resume (Chapter 22).

☐ Start off the school year strong. Know that GPA is the first thing that all colleges look at and consider.

☐ Plan to attend a college fair to get more information and learn more about your future colleges. NACAC (and many high schools) sponsor college fairs in cities across the country during the fall and spring. To learn more about the NACAC fairs, visit www.nationalcollegefairs.org for dates and locations.

September   Designing Your Future

☐ Write down your goals for the year: academic, athletic, work, extra-curricular, etc. (Chapter 8).

☐ Schedule a meeting with your counselor to discuss dual-credit courses you can take next year.

☐ Discuss with your parents the careers that might interest you and see if they have any friends or relatives in that field with whom you can speak about their careers (Chapter 11).

☐ Make concrete plans to join projects/activities that allow you to develop time-management, communication, and leadership skills.

☐ Develop a standardized testing schedule (which tests you will take and when you will take the SAT/ACT) for the entire year (Chapter 15).

☐ Look to take courses such as Honors, AP, or college level courses to challenge you.

☐ Review study materials for the PSAT. You might qualify as a National Merit Semi-finalist or Finalist based on how you do on the (NMSQT) National Merit Scholarship Qualifying Test (Learn more in Chapter 15).

October College Preparation

- ☐ Determine your path to earning a post-secondary degree.

- ☐ Try to visit many different types of colleges to get a feel for what is available to you: large, small, public, and private (Chapter 20).

- ☐ Write down colleges that pique your interest and why you find them appealing (Chapter 21).

6

November Becoming a Balanced Student

- ☐ Look for ways to be involved in a sport or other extra-curricular activities in the winter and spring months.

- ☐ Find ways to build your student resume (Chapter 22) by joining a service project and improving your leadership skills.

- ☐ Build your student resume by joining a service project and improving your leadership skills (Chapter 22).

- ☐ If possible, start a business or non-profit organization. Use these opportunities to explore possible careers and make new friends.

- ☐ Continue to add to your Student Activities Record (Chapter 12) and Awards & Recognitions (Chapter 13).

- ☐ Make it a point to read something new every day. Reading and problem solving are essential skills to master for your future.

December Capitalize on Your Time Off

☐ Select your career interest that you would like to pursue after high school graduation (Chapter 11).

☐ Focus in on a postsecondary path after high school.

☐ Become familiar with any words or terms associated with college admissions with which you might not be familiar (Chapter 27).

☐ Look for opportunities to speak with friends/relatives about their college experiences.

☐ Participate in a school, religious or community holiday service project.

☐ Continue to schedule your college visits for the rest of the year and watch virtual tours before scheduling these visits when available (Chapter 20).

☐ Consider taking on a part-time job so that you can save money for college.

☐ Update your student resume (Chapter 22).

☐ Narrow down your college list (Chapter 21).

☐ Be honest with yourself and ask for help if you need assistance on a particular subject from teachers, mentors, tutors, and schedule extra study sessions.

☐ Continue to meet with and talk to adults you admire about their college and career paths.

☐ Check your GPA and make sure you are on target.

January	Money Matters

☐ Take time to learn more about the difference between the Free Application for Federal Student Aid (**FAFSA**) and the College Scholarship Profile (**CSS Financial** Aid **Profile**) financial aid forms and how they are used to calculate your EFC number (Chapter 16).

☐ If you have not already done so, calculate your *Expected Family Contribution* (EFC) number using either the www.FAFSA4caster.com website or the EFC calculator on the www.collegeboard.org website (Chapter 16).

6

☐ If possible, open a checking account and/or savings account and start to manage your personal finances.

☐ Research who received college scholarships from your high school and write down their accomplishments and all the activities in which they were involved (Chapter 19). Try to identify what made them stand out?

☐ Have your parents determine their credit score by using a FREE credit score calculator.

☐ If you have not already done so, talk with your parents about how much they can afford to put toward helping pay for your college education on an annual or monthly basis. Remember, college can run as much as $16,000 per year for an in-state public university to more than $65,000 per year for a private college.

☐ Start to identify SAT II Tests (If your future colleges expect or strongly recommend you take them) that you may want to take in the coming months. Better to take them when the subject matter is still fresh in your mind.

February — Monitor Your Direction

☐ This is a good time to check your GPA-grade point average (un-weighted and weighted), class rank, and attendance record again (Chapter 10).

☐ Review your yearly goals to see if you are on track to meet them. Do you need to adjust your behavior or attitude to reach the goals you set for yourself? Do you need to make new habits or follow a new path? Are you making good decisions about your future (Chapter 8)?

☐ If you have not already done so, create an email account that you can use for communicating with colleges and submitting private college scholarship applications.

☐ Pay particular attention to your online accounts and clean up your image if necessary. Remember, many colleges check these accounts.

☐ Prepare for SAT/ACT tests and continue your testing strategy (Chapter 15).

March — Academic & Curriculum Strategy

☐ Make sure you are taking the required courses needed for college admissions. Remember, these requirements and expectations can be different the more competitive the college.

☐ Consider volunteering, studying or taking a trip abroad, taking an online course, or enrolling in a summer course at a local community college.

☐ Meet with your counselor to set up your senior year courses. Register for honors, advanced and/or dual credit courses when appropriate.

☐ Plan your electives for 12th grade.

April	Research and Preparation

☐ Do your best on your end-of-year or course tests.

☐ Find study classes, online resources, or guide books to help you with your standardized tests.

☐ Plan ahead for AP/IB exams by finding out more about the tests.

☐ Continue your college visits (Chapter 20).

☐ Begin your search for private scholarships (Chapter 23).

☐ Continue to narrow down your college list (Chapter 21).

☐ Identify individuals who will write your Letters of Recommendation (Chapter 22).

6

May	Adapt and Adjust

☐ Update your college resume (Chapter 22) with the items you have accomplished this year.

☐ Consider attending summer camps or programs that will help you get ahead in school or expand your mind.

☐ Find a summer internship or job shadow related to your future career and college major.

☐ If you are applying to colleges that require the Common Application or Coalition Application (Chapter 24), print off the NEW Essay Prompts and start writing your essay (Chapter 23).

| **Summer** | All About Autumn |

☐ Review your yearly goals to see how you did (Chapter 8).

☐ Decide what you would like to accomplish or achieve over the summer and make plans.

☐ Attend summer camps or activities that will help you grow as a person, find new friends, or learn something new.

☐ Stay active during the summer: physically and mentally.

☐ Review your monthly budget to see how you are doing (Chapter 17).

☐ Find a way to earn extra money: a part-time job, start a small business, identify ways to increase your allowance. Be creative and take action!

☐ Work on a local community service project. Focus on helping others and improving your leadership skills (Chapter 12).

☐ Narrow down your college list (Chapter 21).

☐ Review admission application requirements for schools on your college short list (Chapter 24).

☐ Use college websites to research more colleges or universities that interest you and plan a visit to them ASAP (Chapter 20).

☐ Review admission application requirements on your college short list (Chapter 24).

☐ Decide if you will be applying Early Decision, Early Action, or Regular Admission, and note the deadline dates (Chapter 24 and 27).

☐ Start your college applications (when they go live), continue to work on your essays, and update your resume (Chapter 23).

☐ Continue to save for college (Chapter 17).

☐ Review your EFC number and know which type of financial aid (e.g., merit, need-based, tuition discounts) you will qualify for in the future (Chapter 16).

☐ Continue to search and apply for private scholarships (Chapter 19).

☐ Register for your senior year ACT/SAT, and additional SAT II Tests you plan to take. (If any of your colleges expect or strongly recommend you take them.) Be sure to check Application Deadlines carefully (Chapter 24).

☐ Focus on your primary essay and get it as close to finished as possible, having English Teachers; parents etc. review it along the way (Chapter 23).

☐ Print out last year's version of the Common Application so that you know what to expect when you start completing it when it goes live (Chapter 24).

☐ Be prepared to take action in the fall. You want to be at the top of the pile, not the bottom when colleges are deciding on admissions and scholarships.

6

55

12th Grade Organizational Timeline

"If what you did yesterday seems big, you haven't done anything today".

- Lou Holtz, Coach

August	Exploring Who You Are

Make sure you have completed the following items:

☐ A career profile/personality search (Chapter 11) to identify potential careers available to you.

☐ Identify the careers you feel you will excel in and enjoy (Chapter 11).

☐ Pick a major that will prepare you for your future career path.

☐ Connect again with the individuals you asked back in May about writing you a Letter of Recommendation. Give them a copy of your resume to help them know all that you have accomplished.

☐ Finalize your list of colleges (short list) you plan to apply to AND research the applications you will use to apply to each school and start them as soon as they go live (Chapter 21). Know the applications deadlines.

☐ Start on supplemental essays required by any of your colleges (Chapter 23).

☐ Finalize your college resume (Chapter 22).

☐ Continue to review study materials for future SAT/ACT tests (Chapter 15).

☐ Attend financial aid workshops in your area or seek out assistance from college financial aid experts.

☐ Start off the school year strong. Know that GPA is the first thing all colleges look at and consider in the admissions process, so get your composite GPA, ASAP.

7

September   Designing Your Future

☐ Write down your goals for the year: academic, athletic, work, extra-curricular, etc. (Chapter 8).

☐ Complete your College Applications and Financial Aid Forms by each colleges deadline (Chapter 24).

☐ Follow up on having Letters of Recommendation turned into your counselor or when requested, sent directly (via email or postage) to colleges or scholarship committees on your behalf.

☐ Ask a parent, guardian, counselor and/or college planner to review all of your college applications before submitting them (Chapter 24).

☐ Begin completing college scholarship applications (college specific and private) that are due in the fall (Chapter 19).

☐ Request a copy of your high school transcript and records to check for errors (Chapter 10). Follow your high school's protocol to have official copies sent to your colleges.

☐ Continue to review study materials for future SAT/ACT tests (Chapter 15).

☐ Visit colleges you have not had the opportunity to visit (Section 20).

☐ Get your student and parent FSA ID (Federal Student Aid ID) at: www.fafsa.ed.gov (Chapter 24).

☐ Continue completing and submitting scholarship applications (Chapter 19).

October	College Preparation

☐ It's FAFSA and CSS Profile Time! Check with your final colleges to see which forms they expect you to complete to apply for financial aid. Seek out help in advance if you or your family are not comfortable completing these important forms (Chapter 24).

☐ Make sure you have your FSA ID's (student and parent) ready to use when you start to complete your FAFSA (Chapter 24).

☐ Continue completing your college applications and note early application deadlines! (Chapter 24).

7

☐ Still undecided on a major or college choice? Not to worry, take the time to speak with parents, guidance counselors, and college advisers who can help you discover your future calling and narrow down your search.

☐ Continue to visit colleges you have not had the opportunity to visit so that you can make sure they are a good fit for you (Chapter 20).

☐ Follow on Twitter and Facebook all the colleges on your short list.

☐ Continue to attend College Fairs to get more information about your future colleges and connect with each school's Admissions Representative. To find NACAC fairs, visit www.nationalcollegefairs.org for dates and locations.

☐ Continue completing and submitting scholarship applications (Chapter 19).

November — Becoming a Balanced Student

☐ Try to have all your college applications completed by the end of the month (Chapter 24). If you smell turkey, it may be too late!

☐ Request your SAT and/or ACT test results be forwarded to your college choices (Chapter 15).

☐ Check financial aid deadlines for any schools to which you applied Early Action (EA) or Early Decision (ED), to see if the schools require you to complete the financial aid forms in November (Chapter 24).

☐ Continue completing and submitting scholarship applications (Chapter 19).

☐ Log into the websites (or call if necessary) of the colleges you have applied to and make sure they have received everything they need to process your application (all required materials for a completed application).

December — Capitalize on Your Time Off

☐ If not accepted for early admission, decide if you would like to apply to any more schools. Submit any final college applications (Chapter 24).

☐ If deferred by a college, try to send a letter sharing any NEW updated information (ex. SAT/ACT scores) or accomplishments since you applied.

☐ Look for opportunities to speak with friends/relatives about their college experiences.

☐ If necessary, for college admissions or scholarship qualifications, take the SAT and/or ACT one last time.

☐ Remember your GPA still matters, so finish strong!

January	Money Matters

☐ Complete any outstanding requirements for the CSS Profile as soon as possible (Chapter 24).

☐ Ask your parents to complete their taxes as early as possible this year.

February	Monitor Your Direction	7

☐ Check the status of your financial aid forms and submit any forms that are still outstanding (Chapter 24).

☐ Review the Student Aid Report (SAR) for any errors and make corrections if necessary (Chapter 25).

☐ Continue to search and apply for local scholarships (Chapter 19).

☐ Look for the official financial aid award letters to begin arriving in late February from some of your colleges (Chapter 26).

☐ Review your yearly goals to see if you are on track to meet them. Do you need to adjust your behavior or attitude to reach the goals you set for yourself? Do you need to make new habits or follow a new path? Are you making good decisions about your future (Chapter 8)?

March Academic & Curriculum Strategy

☐ If you received any rejection letters, look to apply to other schools or send more information.

☐ If available and/or necessary, ask your counselor to send in your mid-year high school report card if your GPA has improved AND your college will accept the new GPA.

☐ Await financial aid award letters from all of your outstanding colleges and/or view them on the school's website if available (Chapter 26).

April Research and Preparation

☐ Continue to receive financial aid award letters or view them on each of the school's websites (Chapter 26).

☐ Compare the final cost of all the schools where you have been accepted. This will help you make a wise final college selection (Chapter 26).

☐ If possible, review award letters and when appropriate, appeal for additional financial aid (Chapter 26).

☐ If you are still undecided on where you want to go to college, you may want to visit your top colleges one more time (Chapter 20).

☐ Make your final college choice by May 1st. Schedule your Freshman Orientation date, ASAP.

☐ It is always appropriate to let the other colleges know you have decided not to attend their school.

May	Adapt and Adjust

- [ ] May 1st is National College Decision Day. To lock in your college scholarship at you chosen college you must notify them that you accept it.
- [ ] Decide what other financial aid, if any, you are going to accept.
- [ ] If Waitlisted, get advice to help you make a good decision.
- [ ] Sign-up to take any placement exams.
- [ ] Finish your academic year on a high note. No senioritis!
- [ ] Enjoy the last few weeks of your senior year.

7

Summer	All About Autumn

- [ ] Celebrate your graduation and your accomplishments!
- [ ] Explore and find ways to earn some summer money before you head off to college.
- [ ] Discuss and review all college loan options if necessary.
- [ ] Apply for loans if necessary, complete the required online training, and sign your Loan Promissory Note (Chapter 26).
- [ ] Make out your college packing list and collect everything you are going to need to take to college in the fall.
- [ ] Enjoy your summer break!

Goals and Dreams

"Today I will do what others won't, so tomorrow I can accomplish what others can't."

– Jerry Rice Player

7th Grade

Take a few minutes to write down your future goals and dreams for: academics, athletics, extra-curriculars, work (career), and college.

- _____
  _____
  _____
- _____
  _____
  _____
- _____
  _____
  _____
- _____
  _____
  _____
- _____
  _____

8

8th Grade

Spend some time updating this years goals and dreams for: academics, athletics, extra-curriculars, work (career), and college.

- _____
  _____
  _____
- _____
  _____
  _____
- _____
  _____
  _____
- _____
  _____
  _____
- _____
  _____
  _____

9th Grade

Spend some time updating this years goals and dreams for: academics, athletics, extra-curriculars, work (career), and college.

- _____
  _____
  _____

- _____
  _____
  _____

- _____
  _____
  _____

- _____
  _____
  _____

- _____
  _____
  _____

8

10th Grade

Spend some time reflecting, updating, and exploring this year's goals and dreams for academics, athletics, extra-curricular activities, work (career) and college.

- _____
  _____
  _____
  _____
  _____
  _____
  _____
  _____
  _____
  _____
  _____
  _____
  _____

11th Grade

Continue to research and define your future goals and dreams for academics, athletics, extra-curricular activities, work (career) and college.

- _____

8

12th Grade

Time to take action and make your college and career goals and dreams become a reality. What must YOU do?

- _____
_____
_____
_____
_____
_____
_____
_____
_____
_____
_____
_____
_____

Student Login Details

"I never learn anything talking. I only learn things when I ask questions." - Lou Holtz, Coach

Every time you speak with someone at a college or log into a college website after submitting your application, you will be asked for some general information about yourself. Please take the time to write down your Student ID, Username and/or Password so that you can access this information quickly.

You will also need specific information whenever you log into Financial Aid Websites (FAFSA and CSS Profile) in the future. Use this section to keep track of these login details as well.

COLLEGE LOGIN DETAILS:

Student's Social Security Number:

College # 1 _____ **Student ID and Password:**

College # 2 _____ **Student ID and Password:**

College # 3 _____ **Student ID and Password:**

College # 4 _____ **Student ID and Password:**

College #5 _____ **Student ID and Password:**

College # 6 _____ **Student ID and Password:**

9

FINANCIAL AID LOGIN DETAILS:

FAFSA User Name/Password/Save Key:

STUDENT:

PARENT:

CSS Profile LOGIN Details:

STUDENT:

PARENT:

Continue on to Chapter 10 and take action today!

Remember to visit Coach Dan's website www.collegeandbeyondllc.com and Coach Ryan's website www.collegeaidformiddleclass.com to find additional resources on this important topic!

College selectivity has increased since you were in high school. Aim high, but keep an open mind for schools you have never heard of that might be just right for your student. There are more choices today where your child can grow, be happy, and get a great education. – *Coach Ryan*

Now is the time to take action. No matter where you are in the college process, do something today so that tomorrow you do not have a bunch of regrets! – *Coach Dan*

Report Cards & Unofficial Transcript

"Leadership is more about responsibility than ability!"   — Jim Tunney, Coach

While colleges will not be asking for your report cards, it is a good way to keep track of your progress through middle school and high school. There is a big difference between your **cumulative GPA** and your GPA for each grading period. Please understand the difference, because most colleges are interested in your cumulative GPA for all semesters of high school.

Visually seeing your grades and classes through the years may also help you identify the subject matter that appeals to you most when you are trying to identify what you might want to study in college, or help you understand your **learning style**. For example, you might notice that the classes in which you did best were the ones where the teacher encouraged you to raise your hand in class and interact with other students or where you had a great working relationship with the teacher. These results might suggest your learning style is best suited for a college with smaller classes where you have the opportunity to get to know your professor.

When you start your college admissions applications, request a copy of your **transcript** from your registrar or high school counselor. *By having copies of your Report Cards, you will be able to review your transcript for accuracy.*

Your high school transcript will show your grades, classes taken, credits, and your GPA. It will also likely list your PSAT, SAT or ACT Test Results. This document will probably be the very first item that a college admissions officer will evaluate. The hard work you are putting towards your school work will directly impact your ability to be admitted into colleges. While other elements will also be considered for your college applications, your transcript will show admission officers the difficulty of the classes you are taking, how hard you work, and the areas in which you excel.

10

Transcript

Below are the items that most college admission counselors evaluate on your transcript:

Grade Point Average (GPA): Some schools will look at **weighted GPA**, some will look at **unweighted GPA**, some only consider core classes (math, science, social studies), some look at all your classes, and some schools will use their custom-made formula to calculate your GPA. Students who take Honors, Advanced Placement (AP) and *International Baccalaureate* (IB) classes often receive a "bump up" in their GPA. This weighting is added to the GPA to reflect the difficulty associated with the college prep or college level classes the student takes. For example: a regular Biology class might be on a 4 point scale, versus AP Biology which might be on a 5 point scale. Check with your high school counselors to understand what your high school's grading scale is and what is included on your transcript. Do your research on your future colleges to know what they are going to use (weighted or unweighted) for admissions and scholarship consideration. **IMPORTANT:** some high schools only send out transcripts showing a student's cumulative GPA at the end of their junior year to colleges. **What does your high school do?** You need to know the answer ASAP BECAUSE this could help or hurt you when it comes to qualifying for some scholarships or getting admitted into some of your colleges or universities. Ask today!

Class Rank: According to the National Association for College Admission Counseling (NACAC), 40% of high schools throughout the U.S. do not show a class rank on their transcripts or do not provide it to the colleges. Moreover, more universities are also making it optional for students to include their class rank on the applications. However, some colleges still like to see how the student measures up against their peers.

The Difficulty of Classes: The variety and types of classes you take in high school will help the colleges determine the type of student you are. If a student has taken Honors, AP or IB classes, a college admission counselor will know the student pushed themselves academically.

GPA Fluctuation: As an admission counselor reviews your transcript, not only will they be looking at your classes and GPA, but also to see if you had any grade fluctuation during your high school career. Were you able to take challenging courses and still maintain a high GPA? Did you start your high school career with a low GPA, but you kept working hard to improve it? If you do have a hiccup with your GPA, the vast majority of admission counselors will look at other parts of your application to understand why this grade variation occurred. We also encourage you to take action and share details with the college admissions department to help explain what happened.

> Your high school GPA is one of the first items every college will look at on your application. Yes, grades do matter. *– Coach Ryan*

Other items on your transcript:

Behavior Record: A good behavior record *will not* be on the transcript. However, any suspension or disciplinary reports will be included.

Attendance: Ask your guidance counselor if this is listed.

Other items sent out by your high school counselor with your transcript:

School Profile: This is a general overview of your high school. It will give the college a demographic record of the students, the level of difficulty of the classes offered, Honors/AP/IB

COLLEGE ENTRANCE GAME PLAN

courses offered, the number of students on average who go on to college and other information required by the colleges. When it comes to evaluating a student for the most competitive scholarships, some colleges will look at the rigor of classes a student has taken on their transcript and compare it to what s/he could have taken as noted on the School Profile.

Official Transcript

All colleges expect to receive an **Official Transcript** for each student during the application process and after the student graduates from high school. An *official transcript* will be mailed or sent as a secure (PDF) document electronically from your high school to the college via the application. A transcript is considered "official" when it is "sealed" by the high school, and not tampered with prior to the college admissions department reviewing it.

> Fixing a student's average cumulative GPA is like turning the Titanic. The longer you wait to fix the problem, the more likely you will run into the iceberg. Take action today! Seek out tutoring help or ask if extra credit is available and do it!
> *– Coach Dan*

An **Unofficial Transcript**, on the other hand, exists whenever a transcript has been received by a student, parent or someone else and the "seal" on the envelope has been broken. A college rarely accepts an unofficial transcript from you or your high school. **DO YOUR RESEARCH** to see what your college expects you to send them. *Please ask for a copy of your Unofficial Transcript for your records.*

10

Continue on to Chapter 11 and take action today!

Remember to visit Coach Dan's website www.collegeandbeyondllc.com and Coach Ryan's website www.collegeaidformiddleclass.com to find additional resources on this important topic!

Copyrighted Material © 2016 Ryan Clark and Dan Bisig | 75

Insert your unofficial

Transcript HERE.

Please do not forget to check the transcript for any errors!

Insert your report cards HERE.

Please do not forget to check the transcript for any errors!

10

Career & College Major Search

"Each person holds so much power within themselves that needs to be let out. Sometimes they just need a little nudge, a little direction, a little support, a little coaching, and the greatest things can happen".

\- Pete Carroll, Coach

Did you know that many college students spend an extra one or two years in college because they never took the time to determine their majors before entering college and, in turn, end up changing their majors, sometimes multiple times? Likewise, many students pick fields of study with declining growth trends and are unable to find jobs upon graduation.

One of the most difficult challenges many students face is making decisions about majors and future career paths. They often dread the two questions that every inquisitive friend or family member is inevitably going to ask:

- Where are you going to college?

- What is your chosen major?

One additional question we feel you need to answer is:

- Have you taken the career you are considering for a test-ride by setting up a job shadowing opportunity with a friend, relative, or acquaintance already in the career?

If students take the time to determine the best career fit before entering college, they tend to spend less time in college, which in turn, maximizes the investment (time and money) they spend on getting their education. With a little work and self-reflection, selecting a wise course of study can lead to a lifelong, rewarding career, with personal growth and long-term financial security.

> Research a student's interest and show them all their options that fit their personality and skill set. Don't be surprised if your child is undecided on a career or major. Remember, most careers are not planned, but unfold. If you can narrow their interest into either a Math/Science or Humanities fields, you can narrow your college search. *– Coach Ryan*

11

Though choosing a career path is one of the significant milestones every student faces, change in this modern age is inevitable. On average men change careers within their professional life spans 3 to 4 times while women change 3 to 6 times, so flexibility is key for all students as they prepare for their future. This can be accomplished by focusing on transferable skill sets and similar interests over a set path. The exception to this would be those students who are already laser-focused on going into a pre-professional field (e.g., medicine or law).

To help clarify and answer the second question that has perplexed generations of students and provoked many a sleepless night, we offer the following 5 Step Process:

First Step – Career Interest Inventories and Assessments

We suggest every student completes a Career Interest Inventory and Assessment before entering college. Even if students think they know what they want to study, it is always a good idea to have a backup plan. According to the National Center for Education Statistics, 80 % percent of all students change their major in college. Taking a career assessment will help a student research all possible career fields that fit their skill set, personality, interests, and/or values. Going through this process may reconfirm that a student is on the right career path.

But please note, not all assessments are created equally. Some are free to students, example the assessment done in conjunction with the ACT® Test or as administered by some school districts or states (Career Cruising – ILP or Naviance) and some require a small fee to take their assessment. In other cases, it might make sense to work with a qualified career advisor to do the evaluation (e.g., Living My Purpose or My Career Profile).

We encourage all students to take a few of these assessments during middle school and high school so that as they mature, learn new skills, and discover new interests they can uncover their future career paths. For students who just do not know what they want to do and enter college as "undecided" OR change their minds in college, we recommend that you seek out the career counseling departments on your campuses for additional help and guidance.

Below are a few websites for some of the most popular career interest inventory programs:

Holland Codes: www.hollandcodes.com According to John Holland's theory, most people are one of six personality types: Realistic, Investigative, Artistic, Social, Enterprising, or Conventional.

My Career Planner: http://careerdimensions.com/mcp.php

Self-Directed Search: http://www.self-directed-search.com/

MyPlan: http://www.myplan.com/

MBTI Complete: www.mbticomplete.com

ISEEK.org: http://www.iseek.org/careers/clusterSurvey

My Next Move: www.mynextmove.org

Big Future (College Board): www.bigfuture.collegeboard.org

Myers Briggs: http://www.myersbriggs.org/my-mbti-personality-type/mbti-basics/

Do your homework and decide which of these career interest inventories is best for you; then take the time to do it, review the results, and set a plan of action.

Second Step – Research Careers

After determining the occupations that fit your interests, skills, values, and personality, you need to speak with various people in these particular fields. Speaking with these individuals will allow you to get multiple opinions and learn more about their professions. When contacting these individuals by phone, email, or text, please explain your interest in wanting to determine the benefits of their occupation in a very informal interview. Below are some questions you might want to ask these individuals:

➤ What made you decide to work in this field?
➤ How long have you been in this profession?
➤ Was this your major in college?
➤ What kind of education or training is needed for this profession?
➤ How did you get your first job in this field?
➤ How has it changed over the years?
➤ What do you think the future holds for this occupation?
➤ What do you like the most about your job?
➤ What do you like least about your job?
➤ What are your daily responsibilities and duties?
➤ What does a typical day look like?
➤ What does it take to advance in this career?
➤ What magazines or trade publications do you recommend I read to do more research?
➤ Are there any "hot-button" issues of which I should be aware?
➤ What advice do you have for a high school student interested in studying your field of study?

11

Third Step – More Research

It is not uncommon for recent college graduates to find that the careers they choose do not provide the mental and physical stimulation, nor the financial reward they were expecting based on the hard work they did in college. With college costs skyrocketing, it is essential to get as much information as possible about a potential career field. Take the time during middle school and high school to start the process of exploring potential careers.

• Do your homework on the careers or majors you are considering. You may want to use the internet to do some additional research!

- Try to set up job shadowing opportunities with the help of your parents or high school guidance counselors so that you can learn more about the jobs that interest you.
- Definitely plan to do an internship or co-op in college to take your future career for a test ride-the earlier the better. It's better to find out you don't like it earlier in the college process than to spend 4 or 5 years getting a degree and then discovering when you start your job that you can't stand what you are doing.
- In high school, consider doing summer programs, volunteer opportunities, mini-classes, or part-time jobs that are related to your potential future career. For example, if you are interested in zoology, veterinary studies or marine biology, look into volunteering at the zoo, at a veterinarians' office or at an aquarium in your area.
- Finally, it never hurts to take a class or two in high school in an area that interests you (e.g., landscape design, computer science, photography) to see if that class sparks your future career interests.

Research Occupational Information:

O*Net Online: www.onetonline.org

United States Department of Labor - Occupational Outlook Handbook: http://www.bls.gov/ooh/

The Riley Guide: http://www.rileyguide.com/careers.html

Fourth Step – Rank Your Careers

List all careers that interest you below and rank them with your first choice at the top. You can use the results to help narrow down your colleges when you complete your college selection.

1. _____

2. _____

3. _____

4. _____

Now that you have ranked your potential careers, it is time to go back over them and compare the similarities and differences between each of these fields. Take the time to break down broader fields into sub-categories if necessary. For example, the study of medicine could lead to a student becoming a doctor, RN, physician's assistant, nurse practitioner, physical therapist, or pharmacist). Do your research.

Fifth Step – Take Action

Take the time TODAY to get to know your career likes and dislikes and remember **NOT TO PROCRASTINATE!** The longer you wait to take action the harder it gets to make a career and college decision!

And remember, it is OK to change your mind along the way. By doing these types of career interest inventories, you can knock out 80 to 90% of the careers you have absolutely NO interest in pursuing. Narrow down your potential majors/careers so that you can ultimately map out your future path.

IF after going through this entire process, you still do not know what to choose as a major, then maybe you should consider one of the following options:

- **Maybe** start off at a community of junior college, taking some general education classes (which are applicable, regardless of your future major), and one or two classes in a topic/major you are considering. This will give you the time you need to continue to explore what major/career you want to pursue. By doing well in your classes, you will have choices: either transfer to a 4-year institution where you can finish your major OR complete your 2-year Associates Degree and enter the workforce. The choice will be yours.

> Take the time during middle school and high school to explore potential careers. Better to figure out what you do not want to do AND narrow your choices down so that you attend the right colleges. Heading off to college undecided is not uncommon BUT eventually a decision needs to be made. Choose wisely so that in the future you do not become a statistic (37% of students end up transferring colleges). *– Coach Dan*

11

- **OR** after narrowing down your potential major/career list, identify and attend a college or university offering a broad array of majors that interest you so that when you ultimately decide what major to pursue, you can stay at that same school.
- **OR** consider going to a liberal arts college which allows a student to take classes in many disciplines: arts, social sciences, mathematics, natural sciences, and humanities. A liberal arts degree is generally meant to prepare students for a variety of career paths versus a specific career path. Some schools allow students to create their own major based on their individual interests too!

In all cases, make it a point to visit your college's career counseling department. They are there to help you take additional career interest inventory assessments and give you guidance on how to match your aptitude, interests, skills, values, and personality to a future major and career path. Utilize these services, because you are paying for them as part of your tuition.

Continue on to Chapter 12 and take action today!

Remember to visit Coach Dan's website www.collegeandbeyondllc.com and Coach Ryan's website www.collegeaidformiddleclass.com to find additional resources on this important topic!

Student Activity Record

"Talent is God given. Be humble. Fame is man-given. Be grateful. Conceit is self-given. Be careful."
—John Wooden, Coach

Complete the below **Activity Record** for any extracurricular activities in which you have participated during high school. Make sure you indicate all leadership positions you have held. *Make as many copies as necessary to list all of your activities so that you can keep track of everything.*

School Activities / Community Service / Summer Activities / Work Experience / Sports (circle one)

- ➢ Activity Name/ Employer:_____

- ➢ Description:_____

  _____

  _____

- ➢ Grades Participated (9th, 10th, 11th, 12th):_____

- ➢ Start Date and End Date: _____

- ➢ Time Spent in hours per week: _____

- ➢ Time Spent in hours per year: _____

- ➢ Position(s) or Role: _____

- ➢ Other Information: _____

_____

_____

_____

12

School Activities / Community Service / Summer Activities / Work Experience / Sports (circle one)

> Activity Name/ Employer:_____

> Description:_____

    _____

    _____

> Grades Participated (9th, 10th, 11th, 12th):_____

> Start Date and End Date: _____

> Time Spent in hours per week: _____

> Time Spent in hours per year: _____

> Position(s) or Role: _____

> Other Information: _____

_____

_____

_____

_____

_____

_____

_____

School Activities / Community Service / Summer Activities / Work Experience / Sports (circle one)

- ➤ Activity Name/ Employer:_____

- ➤ Description:_____

  _____

  _____

- ➤ Grades Participated (9th, 10th, 11th, 12th):_____

- ➤ Start Date and End Date: _____

- ➤ Time Spent in hours per week: _____

- ➤ Time Spent in hours per year: _____

- ➤ Position(s) or Role: _____

- ➤ Other Information: _____

_____

_____

_____

_____

_____

_____

_____

12

School Activities / Community Service / Summer Activities / Work Experience / Sports (circle one)

> Activity Name/ Employer:_____

> Description:_____

  _____

  _____

> Grades Participated (9th, 10th, 11th, 12th):_____

> Start Date and End Date: _____

> Time Spent in hours per week: _____

> Time Spent in hours per year: _____

> Position(s) or Role: _____

> Other Information: _____

  _____

  _____

  _____

  _____

  _____

  _____

  _____

School Activities / Community Service / Summer Activities / Work Experience / Sports (circle one)

➢ Activity Name/ Employer:_____

➢ Description:_____

_____

_____

➢ Grades Participated (9th, 10th, 11th, 12th):_____

➢ Start Date and End Date: _____

➢ Time Spent in hours per week: _____

➢ Time Spent in hours per year: _____

➢ Position(s) or Role: _____

➢ Other Information: _____

_____

_____

_____

_____

_____

_____

_____

12

Continue on to Chapter 13 and take action today!

Outside activities are very important and are sometimes as important as your essay, school work, or standardized test scores. Try to focus on a few that you enjoy, excel at, and do well.
– *Coach Ryan*

Better to take the time today to track everything a student is involved in than to wait until the last minute and forget important details. – *Coach Dan*

Remember to visit Coach Dan's website www.collegeandbeyondllc.com and Coach Ryan's website www.collegeaidformiddleclass.com to find additional resources on this important topic!

Awards & Recognition

"Set your goals high, and don't stop until you get there."　　　　- Bo Jackson, Player

Congratulations! You should be very proud of all that you have accomplished. Keeping track of the various awards and recognition you receive starting in the 9th grade can be a big job. Please remember, it is easier to track your awards and accomplishments along the way versus trying to pull it all together in your senior year.

This tab will help you organize your thoughts and make sure none of your accomplishments have been left out as you begin applying for colleges. Having a centralized location to put all of these items will save you a lot of time and help to reduce stress. That is why you need to put all of your awards and recognition in one place in your *College Entrance Game Plan* **Binder**.

> "Who's Who among American High School Students" and "National Youth Leadership Forum" and many other organizations are not really considered honors.
> *– Coach Ryan*

We encourage you to purchase some Binder Pockets or Page Protectors to put in this section of your binder.

As you receive awards and recognition for your accomplishments in the future, put them into theses transparent sleeves. By storing your awards in a single location, you can easily reference them in the future when you need them to complete your college, honors program, and scholarship applications.

13

When it comes to listing your awards and recognition on your applications, start with the most prominent items first, those that will get the attention of any admissions or scholarship person.

Remember, first impressions mean everything!

Continue on to Chapter 14 and take action today!

> Students, be proud of what you have accomplished based on your hard work and community service. Remember, scholarship committees love to see focused individuals who gave back to their community.
> – *Coach Dan*

Remember to visit Coach Dan's website www.collegeandbeyondllc.com and Coach Ryan's website www.collegeaidformiddleclass.com to find additional resources on this important topic!

Insert page protectors or binder pockets after this page.

13

93

AP, CLEP, and DSST Exams & Results

"Never quit. It is the easiest cop-out in the world. Set a goal and don't quit until you attain it. When you do attain it, set another goal, and don't quit until you reach it. Never quit."

– Bear Bryant, Coach

AP: Many students take AP (**Advanced Placement**) exams with the hopes of earning college credit and/or meeting the recommended or expected admissions requirements at top colleges. In fact, some students start taking these exams as early as their freshman year of high school, although your high school may not allow you to take AP courses prior your sophomore or even junior year. In the vast majority of cases, students take an intense year-long class and then take the AP exam in May, which is scored on a scale of 0 to 5. Many colleges give credit for a 4 or 5 on the exam and some even give college credit for a 3. However, you need to do your research by checking on college websites to confirm if they will give you credit for certain scores or specific exams.

While credit policies vary from school to school, AP scores do show every college your academic ability in that particular subject matter. College admissions officers will look at the scores if a student lists the scores on the application. Please note that colleges do not require AP scores to be listed on a college application because not every high school offers AP courses. Since both AP and IB tests measure your knowledge of the most challenging classes and simulate real college courses and tests, schools will sometimes weigh these even more heavily than the SAT and SAT II subject tests. A good grade on an AP or IB test can counteract less than stellar SAT/ACT scores. AP exams can play an important role in admissions, regardless of whether you receive college credit for a particular course from a college.

These exams are often expected if a student is going to meet the admissions requirements for some of the most selective colleges in America. Many of these most selective colleges expect a student to get a 4 or even a 5 to receive college credit for a class. If you apply to an extremely selective college, and you score less than a 4 on an AP test, you should not report the score or list it on your application because it will not help you with admissions. If the university does not offer credit for a 4 or 5 score on an AP test, the college will usually provide the student a wider range of course selection because of their demonstrated mastery of the subject.

> College selectivity has increased since you were in high school. Aim high, but keep an open mind for schools you have never heard of that might be just right for your student. There are more choices today where your child can grow, be happy, and get a great education. *– Coach Ryan*

14

CLEP: Would you be surprised to learn that, in addition to the AP Exams, the College Board also sponsors **College Level Examination Program (CLEP)** exams? There are 33 different CLEP exams in 5 subject areas which also allow a student to qualify for college credits. That's right; there is another way to receive college credit! In fact, we encourage all students to find out more about the various CLEP exams and see if the colleges to which they are applying to will accept CLEP scores. If your college does accept CLEP scores, it is an excellent way to help lower the costs of college by reducing the number of college credits that are required to graduate. *As with the AP Exams, make sure you do your research to confirm if your future college accepts CLEP exams for college credit.*

Additionally, if a student took an AP test and did not receive a high enough qualifying score to receive college credit on the AP exam, then the student should check to see if s/he can take a CLEP exam and still earn college credit. Unlike AP exams that are given one time in May during the school year, CLEP Exams can be taken every three months.

CLEP exams are an excellent way to earn college credit, reduce the cost of college, and offer another alternative to students who did not score high enough on their AP test to receive college credit. Moreover, you can take an AP Exam or a CLEP Exam WITHOUT taking an AP Class.

Students, if there is a subject in which you excel, why not consider taking a CLEP exam to SEE if you can get college credit.

Side note: A student took advantage of a CLEP exam in July of her junior year. After working very hard all year in her AP European History class with a perfect GPA, she ended up only earning a 2 on the AP exam. As you can imagine, she was devastated, needing a 3 to 5 to qualify at most colleges for credit. We encouraged her to consider taking a CLEP exam as a possible alternative to the AP test. She checked her future college website, confirmed they would accept the CLEP exam she planned to take, and scheduled the exam at a local college testing center. After a week of preparation, she took and passed the exam, earning three credit hours at her chosen university! Talk about turning a negative into a positive! Her hard work paid off and in the end she felt vindicated. **DO NOT GIVE UP HOPE!** If you do not score high enough to get college credit on an AP exam, do your research and see if a CLEP exam will work!

DSST: "**DANTES**" or D-S-S-T stands for the **D**efense Activity for Non-traditional Education **S**ubject **S**upport **T**est. Originally, this was a test developed for active military and veterans to get college credit for knowledge without spending time in class. This test is now available to the general public and allows a student to gain college credit from reading, on-the-job training, and independent study. Currently, over 2,000 colleges and universities award college credit for passing scores on the DSST. Much like the AP tests and CLEP tests, the DSST is a wonderful way to save time and money when it comes to college costs. The main difference between the DSST and the CLEP is that the DSST includes more subjects for higher-level learning. Business, Mathematics, Applied Technology, Social Studies, Physical Science, and Social Science are just a few of the 38 tests you can take. Prometric is the company responsible for DSST testing and charges $80 per test. The testing center might also charge an administration fee as well.

BOTTOM LINE: These tests are a wonderful way to save time and money in higher education. **However**, before taking any of these tests, please make sure you confirm the course credit is aligned with your educational goals and that the college(s) you are considering will indeed accept them and give you college credit. **NOT all colleges and universities do.**

REMEMBER you can take an AP Exam, a CLEP Exam, and/or DSST test WITHOUT taking an AP Class. Students, if there is a subject in which you excel, why not consider taking one of these exams to see if you can get college credit. It may be the best money you ever spend!

> More schools (even the Ivy's) are starting to understand that having students push themselves to the brink by taking a rediculous number of AP or IB classes isn't always healthy. Choose wisely!
> - *Coach Dan*

Continue on to Chapter 15 and take action today!

14

> Remember to visit Coach Dan's website www.collegeandbeyondllc.com
> and Coach Ryan's website www.collegeaidformiddleclass.com
> to find additional resources on this important topic!

AP, CLEP, and DSST Exam Tracking Sheet

Test Type (AP, CLEP, DSST)	Exam Name/Subject	Score	Credit

Standardized Tests, Prep and Results

"Success comes from knowing that you did your best to become the best that you are capable of becoming."
- John Wooden, Coach

When it comes to college, ONE of the many items used by college admissions officers to determine which students to admit and give scholarships to are Standardized Tests. Regardless of the colleges you plan to apply to in the future, taking these tests seriously and prepping for them can make all the difference in the world. Let's take a minute to talk about each of them:

ACT Aspire

Aspire is a suite of tests for assessing Common Core performance in English, math, reading, science, and writing. It can be given every year starting in the 3rd grade all the way through 10th grade, to assess student growth. The test will use ACT benchmarks to determine college readiness. The content is the same as the ACT; however the Aspire test is different because of the variety of question types: multiple choice, short answer, or long answer, essays and narratives.

PreACT

PreACT (replacement for the PLAN) can be administered anytime from September 1 through June 1 in the 10th grade that includes shorter versions of the ACT: English, Math, Reading, and Science sections, but it will not include the optional essay section. It will provide "predictive scores" on the ACT's familiar 1-36 score scale.

PSAT - Preliminary SAT – National Merit® Scholarship Qualifying Test (NMSQT)

This test is taken by students in their junior year of high school (and as a practice by some sophomores). Modeled after the SAT, the PSAT has a score range of 320 to 1520. Students are tested in reading and writing, and also math. Scores from both sections are added together to come up with a final composite score. Approximately 7,400 finalists are ultimately selected to receive scholarships which range from The National Merit® $2,500 Scholarship, corporate sponsored scholarships, and college sponsored merit scholarship awards.

ACT® – American College Testing Program or American College Test

This standardized college entrance exam is also used by many colleges for admissions. This test is considered content-based and students are tested in 4 areas: English, math, reading and science. Each section is scored based on a range of 1 to 36 and the sections are averaged together to come up with a final composite score. The highest possible score a student can receive is a 36. The maximum number of times a student can take the ACT is 12; however, the most selective colleges take notice of how many times a student takes this exam and may expect to see every test score.

- The essay is optional BUT do your research to see if the college(s) to which you are applying require it. The essay is scored by 2 different people on a scale of 2-12 (with a 3rd reader if the scores are too far apart) based on four writing domain scores: Ideas and Analysis, Development and Support, Organization, and Language Use and Conventions, each scored on a scale of 2-to-12.

SAT® – Scholastic Aptitude Test

This standardized college entrance exam is administered by the College Board and is used by many colleges for admissions. Redesigned and launched in its NEW format in March 2016, this test is said to correspond more closely to high school curriculums and better reflect what students have learned. There are two sections: Math and Evidence-Based Reading and Writing. Each section is scored on a range of 200 to 800 and both scores are added together for a final composite score. The maximum score is a 1600. There is no limit to the number of times a student can take the test, however, the most selective colleges take notice of how many times a student takes it and may expect to see every test score. Wrong answers DO NOT count against a student's final score.

- The essay is optional BUT do your research to see if your future college(s) requires it for admissions.

- The essay is scored by 2 different people. Each scorer awards 1–4 points for each dimension: reading, analysis, and writing.

- The two scores for each dimension are added together.

- Students receive three scores for their SAT Essay, one for each dimension — ranging from 2–8 points.

SAT® Subject Tests

In addition to standardized test scores (ACT and SAT), approximately 160 colleges expect a student to take SAT Subject Tests to confirm their mastery of specific subjects: science, English, math, history, and foreign languages, and only require two Subject Tests of your choosing. The content of these tests evolves based on current trends in high school course work as determined by the College Board. There are 20 Subject Tests available so check your college website(s) to see IF they require SAT Subject Tests and which tests they recommend or expect you to take to fulfill their test requirements. Colleges that require these tests will also accept the ACT in lieu of SAT Subject Tests. There is still one college that requires three Subject Tests at this time. It is important to check, as testing requirements do change.

TOEFL – Test of English as a Foreign Language

The TOEFL Test is used to evaluate the English proficiency of students whose native language is not English. The format of this exam is multiple-choice and is given in one-three hour session. Three sections must be completed: Listening Comprehension, Structure and Written Expression, and Vocabulary and Reading Comprehension.

Do your research to see if your future colleges expect a student to take the TOEFL test and also the score they expect you to receive to meet their admissions requirements. Go to www.toefl.org to learn more.

Superscore:

Some colleges and universities will take section scores from different SAT or ACT tests and average them together to come up with a NEW higher average score, versus just going with a student's single highest composite score from one SAT or ACT. If a college superscores, they will record your highest individual section scores from the standardized tests you sent them.

SAT Superscore Example:

- March SAT Test Scores: 650 Math and 510 Writing and Language

- May SAT Test Scores: 710 Math and 550 Writing and Language

- June SAT Test Scores: 680 Math and 600 Writing and Language

In this example, your **superscore** would be a 710 in Math from the May test plus 600 in Writing and Language from the June test making your **SUPERSCORE 1320**.

*While some colleges and universities do superscore, some schools still only consider the best score for any one test date. Also note that some colleges ONLY superscore the SAT and NOT the ACT or vice versa, some only superscore for admissions, others ONLY for scholarships, and others for both. **Please check with your specific colleges to determine if they will superscore your SAT and/or ACT and what they use this score for.**

When should you take the ACT/SAT?

Sophomore Year – Critical IF you are planning to apply to Elite Colleges

Test	Dates	Comment
PSAT	*October*	ONLY offered this month and TRULY is a Practice Test
PreACT or Aspire	Fall or Spring?	As scheduled by the school
SAT Subject Test	May or June	Courses in which you will not take a higher level in high school. Example: World History, Biology, Chemistry, etc.
Diagnostic Test or first SAT/ACT	March - June	Diagnostic Tests can help you determine if it is better for you to take the ACT or the SAT. Another alternative is to take both your first SAT and ACT at the end of your sophomore year. This is especially true IF you plan to apply to selective colleges in the future OR have completed advanced math (Algebra I, Algebra II, Geometry, etc.) by the end of your sophomore year. You can determine which test you prefer, get a benchmark score to help with future test preparation, and eliminate the first time test jitters.

Junior Year

If you have not completed a Diagnostic Test or taken the ACT or SAT during your sophomore year, please take both of these tests at least once by the fall/winter of your junior year. Based on your score results, determine which of the tests is best for you to continue to prep for and take. Use an online search engine and type in "SAT/ACT Conversion Chart" to find a good comparison table. **NOTE**: at the time of this publication, this new comparison table (also called the Concordance Table) is still under construction.

If you take the PreACT or Aspire test during your sophomore year and a PSAT test in your sophomore or junior year, you can also use these test results to help you decide if you will do better on the ACT or the SAT in the future. If your scores are approximately the same, choose the test you prefer or are more comfortable taking.

Junior Year Testing

Test	Dates	Comment
PSAT	*October*	Do not think of this as a practice test. If you score high enough, you might qualify for a National Merit Scholarship.
ACT	Sept, Oct, Dec, Feb	Take the ACT
	March	Take another ACT (some states mandate this test)
	April, and June	Take a final ACT
		OR
SAT	Aug (starting 2017-18), Oct, Nov, Dec	Take the SAT
	March	Take another SAT (some states mandate this test)
	May, and June	Take a final SAT

Senior Year Testing

If you are not satisfied with your scores, plan on studying over the summer between your junior and senior years. Focus your efforts on your weakest areas to maximize your test scores.

Test	Dates	Comment
ACT	Sept, Oct, Dec	Take final test(s) if necessary
SAT	Aug (starting 2017-18) Nov, Dec, Jan	Take final test(s) if necessary

*If a student suffers from test anxiety, please seek professional help with strategies to help them.

**If a student has an IEP or 504, please connect with your high school counselor ASAP to follow the necessary steps to get approval of testing modifications, such as getting extended time on the test.

Note: A student from North Carolina applied to seven different colleges during the fall of his senior year. After researching the University of South Carolina's merit aid scholarships, he knew that in order for his family to afford this school and avoid out-of-state tuition costs, he needed to increase his highest ACT composite score by one more point. He took the test in September and then in October hoping to raise his score. Unfortunately, he did not improve his score on either of these tests. He received his Acceptance Letter in December to attend the University of South Carolina, and it motivated him to see if he could try one last time. He found out that USC would indeed accept the February ACT test results and so he decided to take it. Thankfully he achieved the composite score needed and submitted it to the university. His diligence and hard work saved him and his family nearly $100,000 in college costs. Do your homework and identify the last test date your future college(s) will accept for admissions and scholarship contention. Then take the time to prepare for the test and maybe you will achieve your goal as well!

How many times should you take these tests?

This question perplexes many students, partially for fear that their future college will frown on the number of times they took these tests. Check your future college's website or call the admissions office and ask the question. Do not forget, some colleges expect to see ALL of your scores and the costs can add up. So the answer is, it all depends. As you start to select colleges based on how they fit you (academically, financially, socially and geographically), it will become clear what test score(s) you need to achieve in order to have any chance at getting admitted and/or be in the running for the most competitive scholarships. Ideally you want to be in the top 25% of incoming freshman. Do your research, identify the ACT/SAT score you need, and **GO FOR IT!**

Just remember, taking these tests multiple times **WITHOUT** doing some kind of test preparation will lead to frustration when you keep getting the same score on back-to-back tests or possibly even see your score drop. By mapping out a testing and studying schedule, success can be achieved!

Test Optional

More colleges every year are allowing students to apply WITHOUT submitting an SAT or ACT score. Today, over 850 colleges and universities do NOT use these tests to admit students. The trend has accelerated with more and more schools dropping this testing requirement since 2014. You can find a list of schools that are test optional at www.fairtest.org.

Beware, some test optional schools will knock you out of the running for merit scholarships IF you do not submit standardized test scores. Call and ask each school about their policy.

Resources to help you Prepare for the ACT or SAT

15

There are many resources available to prepare for each of these standardized tests. Some are **Free**; while others are **Fee Based**. The KEY is to find the right prep solution for you based on your learning style and what works best for you.

Four primary ways to prepare

1. **Buy a Prep Book**
2. **Do One-on-one Tutoring**
3. **Join a Group Test Prep Program**
4. **Use a Computer Based Tutoring Program**

Below we have listed some popular **Free** and **Fee Based** resources for you to explore and use to improve your test scores.

Free and Inexpensive Test Prep Resources

1. **KHAN Academy** https://www.khanacademy.org This fantastic website offers FREE SAT tutoring as well as some other subjects such as math (all grade levels), science, etc.
2. **Number2.com** http://www.number2.com This is a popular FREE test prep website to help students with SAT or ACT questions and allows students (and parents) to track their progress.
3. **ACT Test Bank by Allen Prep** This app has done all the hard work for you by providing resources to prep for all the ACT subject areas. Practice questions come with detailed explanations of how the right answer was achieved and this program tracks your progress throughout every section of the test. http://itunes.apple.com/us/app/act-testbank-36id439279625?mt=8
4. **INeedAPencil.com** http://www.ineedapencil.com This is a free, comprehensive online SAT prep program that provides dozens of lessons, hundreds of practice questions, and practice exams.
5. **FreeTestPrep.com** http://www.freetestprep.com This website offers a ton of FREE tools to students, including practice questions, video explanations, study guides, ACT/SAT articles, and flashcards. With easy navigation and a no-hassle setup, students can dive right into subject-by-subject quizzes that offer feedback on incorrect answers. With a focus on high quality and student success, FreeTestPrep is a resource for students looking to get an edge on the ACT/SAT.
6. **ACT Student Test Prep** http://www.actstudent.org/testprep This website provides both free and inexpensive ways to prepare for the ACT including, retired exams, diagnostics, content review, practice questions and test-taking tips covering all four sections: Math, Reading, Science, and English. There is also an individual page for the optional essay section.
7. **Official SAT Question of the Day from The College Board.** http://sat.collegeboard.com/practice/sat-question-of-the-day You'll also find links to practice questions and tips for the reading, math, and writing sections, as well as a full-length practice test—all for free.
8. **ACT Question of the Day** http://www.act.org/qotd

9. **Spark Notes** http://www.sparknotes.com/testprep This website provides free diagnostics, practice tests, and flashcards. You'll find a myriad of free test prep resources for the SAT, ACT, and Subject Tests.

10. **MajorTests.com** http://www.majortests.com/sat This website offers a free self-study SAT preparation program, complete with vocabulary word lists, and practice questions for math, writing, and critical reading along with an eight-week guided study plan.

11. **Brightstorm's Online Learning Network** includes low-cost video-based test prep with teaching videos in short, personalized formats as well as practice tests, downloadable materials and comprehensive study guides. More information is available at Brightstorm SAT Test Prep and Brightstorm ACT Test Prep.

12. **Kaplan Test Prep** http://www.kaptest.com Kaplan offers students a wealth of educational help in the form of tutoring and comprehensive courses, but they also offer this gem, a *free* online SAT or ACT practice test with a score review. By registering for one of the online test dates, students can gain a valuable look into what their chosen test will feel like.

13. **ACT test takers,** http://www.actstudent.org/testprep/ Going to the official ACT website can help students learn test taking tips, read descriptions of the subjects tested, view sample questions, and browse through a downloadable booklet that contains a practice test, scoring key, test info, and more.

14. **Adapter: SAT Math by Empire Edge** This iPhone App tracks how you do on the math practice questions, identifies and tracks the errors you make and then offers additional practice questions and gives you further instruction on how to answer those that you miss. http://www.adapster.com

15. **SAT Question of the Day**
https://itunes.apple.com/us/app/official-sat-question-day/id361264754?mt=8

16. For the **SAT takers**, the official College Board website offers study guides, study plans, practice tests, information on what you'll be tested on, and a breakdown of the SAT. Additionally, the SAT site provides a bunch of tips, tricks, strategies, and suggestions on how to study for, and take the entrance exam. https://sat.collegeboard.org

17. In addition to the website mentioned above, there are a number of great Test Prep books available that can supplement the prep work you are doing. Check your local Library or www.amazon.com to identify the best-written resources for you.

Fee Based Test Prep Resources

Real ACT Prep Guide by Princeton Review

- Five practice tests from previous actual test administrations—each with an optional Writing Test
- Explanations for all right and wrong answer choices
- An in-depth look at the optional Writing Test and how it is scored
- Valuable test-taking strategies for each test section: English, Mathematics, Reading, Science, and the optional Writing
- All you need to know about the ACT—formatting, structure, registration, and how colleges interpret your scores
- A review of important topics in English, math, science, and writing
- How to prepare—physically, mentally, and emotionally—for test day

ePrep

15

We added ePrep as part of our college practices years ago because of the fantastic test results students gain from this incredible computer based virtual tutoring program. There are four things that make this test prep program stand out from the rest of the crowd:

(1) Expert Teachers

ePrep video instruction is given by teaching experts. They define an expert teacher as someone who not only commands mastery of the subject material (the so-called "99th percentile scoring instructor) but more importantly, someone who is a master in teaching the subject material to students of all abilities. It's a critical distinction.

(2) Proven Methodology

ePrep study programs employ a proven, results-driven methodology of (1) test, (2) grade, (3) review and (4) repeat. Contrary to popular belief, there are no shortcuts, quick fixes or magic wand solutions to a high SAT, ACT or PSAT score. Any student willing to put in the practice and review can significantly increase their test score. The saying "you make your own breaks" applies to the SAT, ACT and PSAT and most standardized tests.

(3) Simulates Real Conditions

Practicing under simulated test-day conditions is almost as important as knowledge of the subject material. In the same manner, professional athletes and military personnel practice under real-life conditions, your success on the SAT, ACT or PSAT depends on your familiarity with test-day conditions. ePrep deliberately provides paper-based SAT, ACT and PSAT practice tests, which students take sitting at a desk or kitchen table with a timer, so they can emulate the environment they will encounter on test day. Upon completion of the practice tests, ePrep leverages the Internet medium to deliver expert video review and instruction.

(4) Makes Learning Fun and Easy

Learning comes so much easier to students when they are engaged and having fun. ePrep's innovative online video platform, combined with expert instruction, rapidly increases the rate of student learning. ePrep is available by computer 24/7 and is extremely easy to use. More importantly, instead of "telling" a student how to approach a problem through written instruction, ePrep's expert videos "show" a student how to answer each question and also provide keen insights. A student's hard work should be focused on applying learned knowledge, not in obtaining it.

GREAT ACT/SAT Test Taking Tips

1. **DO NOT cram the day before the test**
   Hopefully, you have taken the time to prep for your test. Waiting until the night before to cram will only stress you out so don't do it. Use what you know to do great on the test. Make it a point to get to bed early and wake up early the day of the test.

2. **Grab the items you need for test day the night before**

   The night before your test, go ahead and grab everything you need for test day: an official photo ID, your test admission ticket, an approved calculator (**with new batteries**), a snack and/or water, a watch, and plenty of #2 pencils.

3. **Arrive early on test day**

   Check your test admission ticket to confirm your testing location. Make it a point to arrive early so that you can check in and get ready to take your test. Rushing to get to your testing center will only stress you out so arrive early and do great on your test!

4. **Dress appropriately (in layers)**

   The climate in test centers can vary from sauna-like to frigid. Be prepared for both extremes and everything in-between. You need to be comfortable to do your best.

5. **Pace yourself through the test questions**

   Each question is worth the same number of points. If a question is confusing or too time-consuming, don't lose your cool. Instead, move on to greener pastures. You can come back to hard questions if you have time at the end of a section.

6. **Guessing is OK**

   If you don't know an answer, don't leave the question blank or guess randomly. Eliminate the choices you know are wrong, and then make an educated guess from the remaining options. Remember, if you can eliminate even one answer choice, then it pays to guess.

7. **Pay attention when you are filling in your bubble answer sheets**

   There is nothing worse than discovering somewhere in the exam that you accidentally jumped ahead and are on the wrong question. Check occasionally to make sure you are filing answers next to the right numbers.

8. **Take a deep breath and relax**

   Your attitude and outlook are crucial to your test-day performance. Be confident.

Continue on to Chapter 16 and take action today!

TESTING LOG

ACT Aspire Test:

Date Taken	English Score	Math Score	Reading Score	Science Score	Composite

PreACT Test:

Date Taken	English Score	Math Score	Reading Score	Science Score	Composite

PSAT Test:

Date Taken	Reading/Writing (200-800)	Math (200-800)	Total (400-1600)	Essay (2-8)

109

ACT Test:

Date Taken	English (1-36)	Math (1-36)	Reading (1-36)	Science (1-36)	Composite	Writing (1-36)
Superscore						

SAT Test:

Date Taken	Reading/Writing (200-800)	Math (200-800)	Total (400-1600)	Essay (6-24)
Superscore				

SAT Subject Test:

Date Taken	Subject Name	Score

SAT, PSAT, PreACT, ACT, TOEFL, ISEE, SSAT, HSPT, DSST and AP are registered trademarks not owned by College Entrance Game Plan. The trademark holders were not involved in the production of, and do not endorse, this book.

AP Test:

Date Taken	Subject Name	Score

CLEP Test:

Date Taken	Subject Name	Score

SAT, PSAT, PreACT, ACT, TOEFL, ISEE, SSAT, HSPT, DSST and AP are registered trademarks not owned by College Entrance Game Plan. The trademark holders were not involved in the production of, and do not endorse, this book.

TOEFL Test:

Date Taken	Listening Comprehension	Structure and Written Expression	Vocabulary and Reading	Total Score

Take the time to Print out Your Test Results and add them to your binder!

Make sure you know which test is required by which college, especially at highly selective colleges. SAT Subject Based tests are very common requirements.
– *Coach Ryan*

Parents, if your student struggles with standardized tests, stop and seek out help today. Students, realize that 1 test does NOT define you as a person or the success you can achieve in life! Definitely do everything you can to improve your score so that in the end you can confidently say I gave it my all!
- *Coach Dan*

Remember to visit Coach Dan's website www.collegeandbeyondllc.com and Coach Ryan's website www.collegeaidformiddleclass.com to ORDER the **ePrep Program** or find additional resources!

SAT, PSAT, PreACT, ACT, TOEFL, ISEE, SSAT, HSPT, DSST and AP are registered trademarks not owned by College Entrance Game Plan. The trademark holders were not involved in the production of, and do not endorse, this book.

EFC Calculation

"Success is a journey, not a destination."   Arthur Ashe, Tennis Player

Expected Family Contribution (EFC): This is a dollar amount, determined by the Department of Education, that is used by each school to determine the type and amount of financial aid a student will receive at each institution.

Colleges and universities use the Federal Methodology (FM) and/or the Institutional Methodology (IM) to calculate your EFC number. This dollar amount can be different because FM and IM use slightly different formulas to determine your EFC amount.

To get a better understanding of the Financial Aid Overview, please refer to **Chapter 24**, *where we have listed a few key college planning terms and discussed the Need-based financial aid formula.*

Regardless of your financial situation, completing the Free Application for Federal Student Aid (**FAFSA**) or **CSS**/Financial Aid **PROFILE** should be an important part of your college funding plan. Take the time to submit these forms as soon as they are available so that you do not miss any important deadlines. Meeting these deadlines is very important if you think you will qualify for any **Need-based Financial Aid**. Federal Need Based Aid includes the Pell Grant, SEOG, and Workstudy. In some states and colleges, need-based aid is given out on a first-come, first-served basis so **DO NOT procrastinate**!

PLEASE NOTE: The amount of **Pell Grant, SEOG** and **Workstudy** that a student will be offered depends on the parents' income, non-retirement assets/savings AND the student's income and non-retirement assets/savings.

FAFSA (EFC): The Power of 1 Form

Family B:	
Income:	$60,000
College Savings	$25,000
Other Savings	$25,000
Other real estate:	$50,000
Number in family:	4
Number in school	1
EFC:	$8,295

Family A:	
Income:	$60,000
College Savings	$25,000
Other Savings	$25,000
Other real estate:	$50,000
Number in family:	4
Number in school	1
EFC:	$19,098

How can "Family B" have an EFC number of $8,295 and "Family A" have an EFC number of $19,098 with exactly the same financial and factual information?

One family understood the importance of early EFC planning (Family B) and implemented strategies to reduce their EFC number, and the other family did not (Family A).

Wouldn't it be good to know this EFC number NOW and determine whether or not this amount can be reduced?

Below are a few websites you can use to help calculate your Expected Family Contribution and potential financial aid.

16

Net Price Calculator (NPC)

- Every college has a NPC on their website which will give you an early estimate of how they think you should pay for their college.

FAFSA.ed.gov and then search for FAFSA4caster

- The FAFSA4caster provides an early estimate of your EFC and the type of Federal Financial Aid a student might receive.

collegeboard.com

- Use the EFC calculator on this website to calculate your Federal Methodology (FM) and Institutional Methodology (IM) EFC dollar amounts.

Know What The Colleges Will Expect You To Pay

The colleges and universities will determine what they feel a family can afford to pay towards their student's college education by using what is called the Free Application for Student Aid, better known as the "**FAFSA.**" In addition to using the FAFSA, there are approximately 275 colleges who will require you to complete the **CSS/Financial Aid PROFILE**.

The **CSS Profile** is not used to determine federal or state financial aid; it is used by colleges to distribute their own institutional resources (Endowment Funds). After completing the financial aid applications, the college will tell a student what s/he will qualify for in financial aid. This is very similar to borrowing money from your bank.

For example, when you borrow money for an important purchase, you have to complete a loan application. Once completed, the loan officer will either approve your loan request or deny it. If your loan is denied, the bank will typically tell you why and explain what additional information they need to approve the loan.

The college financial aid forms are similar to those completed when you apply for a loan from a bank. However, neither the college Financial Aid Director nor the federal or state governments will explain to you how they calculated your expected contribution (EFC).

VERY IMPORTANT: You have NO control over what TYPE of financial aid you will receive, nor do you have any control over the AMOUNT. The only people who will dictate these decisions are the Financial Aid Officer at the colleges where your student is applying to in the future.

Knowing how much the colleges will expect parents to contribute toward their student's education is very, very, important. Just like when you borrow money to purchase a new home or other large ticket item, you really need to know exactly how much a college is expecting you to pay. **Only then can you begin to assess whether your family can afford to send your student to a particular college or university.**

Calculate Your Expected Family Contribution

The formula that is used to calculate your family's Federal financial need is called the **FEDERAL METHODOLOGY** (FM) formula. It was adopted by Congress as part of the Higher Education Act of 1986.

Every accredited college and university in the United States uses it to evaluate the eligibility of every student who applies for federal financial aid.

The Federal Methodology determines how much the family is expected to contribute towards their student's college education and the student's eligibility to receive financial aid to cover the remaining balance.

UNDERSTANDING THE CONCEPT OF FINANCIAL NEED

16

The financial aid system presumes that most families can contribute some money towards educational expenses. The amount of money the family is expected to pay is determined by the **FEDERAL METHODOLOGY FORMULA**.

The difference between the amount the family is expected to contribute and the total cost of college represents the student's **FINANCIAL NEED**.

The process of determining a student's **FINANCIAL NEED** is called **NEEDS ANALYSIS**. It is calculated using the following three-line formula:

Total College Cost (COA)
Minus
Family's Contribution (EFC)
Equals
Total Financial Need

This formula establishes the family's eligibility for financial assistance, by which the total amount of aid received by the student cannot exceed the total cost of attending the educational institution.

TOTAL COST OF ATTENDING

The **Total Cost of Attendance (COA)** is a predetermined number, the components of which are detailed in the college catalogs and brochures. The Financial Aid Office labels this as their budget. Before you apply for financial aid, it is imperative that you know the exact costs for each college.

Total costs can be increased by the FAO (Financial Aid Officer) for special purposes, such as special medical or disability expenses.

The Financial Aid Budget or Total Cost of Attending used by most colleges includes the following:

TUITION AND FEES - This number will differ from private colleges and public universities. Tuition is the charge for instruction. Fees include items such as health insurance, library fees, lab fees and other student activity fees.

BOOKS AND SUPPLIES - The cost of books and supplies varies depending on the courses taken. Supplies for the lab, computer, engineering, and art programs may raise the cost significantly.

ROOM AND BOARD - The cost of housing depends on whether the student lives at home, in a student dorm, or off campus. Food costs vary in different areas of the country. A student may choose a school meal plan, eat at home, or cook for themselves.

PERSONAL EXPENSES- Many colleges allow expenses for clothing, insurance, medical care, disability, childcare, personal computer, handicapped provisions and other related items.

TRANSPORTATION – This category includes commuting expenses (bus or cab fare, personal car maintenance, gas, etc.) and round-trip travel during school vacation periods. **NOTE**: The Financial Aid Officer's idea of round-trip travel is usually by bus, not by air. The student must make up the difference.

When analyzing the student's need, some colleges will meet 100% of the student's total financial need and others will meet only a percentage. If the college only meets a percentage of need, it is called **gapping**.

By calculating your potential financial aid need, it can help the student and parents evaluate the colleges (based on potential cost) **BEFORE** applying for admission.

UNDERSTANDING THE EXPECTED FAMILY CONTRIBUTION (EFC)

The Federal Methodology Formula combines hundreds of computations to arrive at the **Expected Family Contribution (EFC)**. The following is a simplistic version of this complex formula.

The Expected Family Contribution (EFC) is computed using the family's financial data submitted on the **Free Application for Federal Student Aid (FAFSA)** application.

This analysis estimates how much the family can be expected to contribute, but makes **NO assumptions about how they will finance that contribution.**

Student's Contribution

- The student's income is assessed at 50% after the first $6,400 of earnings. NOTE: this earnings threshold may increase each year so do your homework.
- The student's assets are assessed at a flat 20%.

Parents' Contribution

- The parents' income is assessed between 22% - 47%, depending on the level of total adjusted gross income.
- Non-taxable income and benefits, such as contributions made during the current year to retirement funds (401K/403B/IRAs) and distributions from non-taxable social security income or other tax-free benefits are added back into the parents' income for assessment.
- The parents' assets (<u>home</u> and <u>family farm</u> **equity are not included)**, minus an asset protection allowance based on the older parent's age, are assessed at 5.65%.

All income from the student and parents is assessed using <u>**year-end tax data from the year preceding**</u> the year when the student enters college. Asset data are listed **as of the date the financial aid forms are filed**.

CALCULATING YOUR EFC - Step By Step

Most families are told to go to the college's website and use a software program to calculate their Expected Family Contribution **(EFC)**. Software programs are a very handy tool and many times simple to use. However, many don't give you a **TRUE** picture of your EFC.

By using the **ACTUAL** formula **(contained in this publication)**, you will be able to calculate your EFC and understand how your income and assets are affecting your potential financial aid eligibility.

Calculating your **Expected Family Contribution** or **EFC** is similar to completing your income tax return. When completing your tax return, the federal and state governments will give you certain deductions **(e.g., mortgage interest payments, charitable contributions, personal exemptions)**, before calculating the amount of tax you owe. When completing the **FAFSA,** you also receive certain deductions that can be applied to your income and assets before calculating your final EFC. Let's look at how you calculate your EFC.

Some of the following information is being provided by the Federal Methodology Formula that was approved by Congress for the school year 2016-2017.

STEP ONE: Adjusted Gross Income (school year 2016-2017)

The calculation of your EFC starts with the student's and parents' **Adjusted Gross Income**. On the FAFSA, there are two sections-one for the student to complete and one section for the parents. The FAFSA will ask the following question in each section:

What was your (and spouse's) adjusted gross income for 2015? Adjusted gross income is on IRS Form 1040, 1040A, or 1040EZ.

Adjusted Gross Income is your total income from earned and unearned income (e.g., **Interest/dividends, capital gains, business earnings, rental/farm income, state income tax refund)** minus certain adjustments to income during the tax year (e.g., **deductible IRA contributions, student loan interest paid, self-employed health insurance premiums, business, capital gains, rental/farm losses).**

TIP: *The lower your Adjusted Gross Income, the more you could qualify for federal, state, and college need-based financial aid. Establishing a home-based business could produce losses that could reduce other taxable income **(e.g., employment/interest/dividend/capital gains) - check with your CPA.** You could use business deductions that could be applied against your business earnings. Using these deductions against earnings could create a tax-free income that could be used to help pay for college expenses.*

TIP: *If you have assets **(e.g., CDs, Money Markets, Mutual Funds, Stocks, and Bonds)** that are producing taxable income, check with your college advisor to evaluate these investments to see if you could put these assets into investment tools that don't produce taxable income. Since state income tax refunds are includable in your Adjusted Gross Income on your federal income tax return the next year, consider increasing your withholding so you **DON'T** get a state income tax refund. **(Talk to your CPA or tax advisor.)***

STEP TWO: Taxes Play an Important Role

The next items that affect your EFC are the amount of taxes **(Federal, State, and Social Security)** you paid on your taxable income. The FAFSA asks you to:

Enter your (and spouse's) income tax for 2015. The income tax amount is on IRS Form 1040, 1040A, or 1040EZ.

Note: Taxes paid on earned and unearned income are deductible against your total income when calculating your EFC. When reading this line on the FAFSA, you will notice that it is **ONLY** asking for Federal Income taxes owed and paid. You will also see that they are not asking how much state or social security taxes you paid during the year.

However, for you to calculate your EFC, **you need to know how much social security and state income taxes you paid during the year.** The Federal Methodology Formula will deduct taxes paid for federal, state and social security taxes. Taxes paid to the state and to social security are found in the formula and are **internal calculations.**

To calculate your EFC, you need to know how this internal calculation is incorporated. Social Security taxes are assessed at 7.65% of earned income. Keep in mind that these income figures could be adjusted each year.   • 6.2% on earned income up to $118,500
• 1.45% on **ALL INCOME**
Total 7.65%

Example: If you earned $80,000, your social security tax is $6,120 **($80,000 X 7.65% = $6,120)**. If you earned $150,000 your social security tax is $9,522 **($118,500 X 7.65% = $9,065 + {$150,000 - $118,500 = $31,500 X 1.45% = $457} = $9,522)**

16

Important Note: *If you invest into a 401-K, you don't pay federal or state income taxes for your contribution. However, the federal government **DOES** withhold social security taxes. When calculating your social security tax deduction, include the social security taxes paid on 401-K contributions.*

Example: If your **taxable income** was $80,000 and you contributed $3,000 into a 401-K plan, calculate your social security tax on the $3,000 401-K contribution, **($80,000 X 7.65% = $6,120 + $3,000 401-K contribution X 7.65% = $230 = $6,350)**.

Since state income tax varies from state to state, the Federal Methodology Formula has a table that it uses to calculate this internal calculation. To calculate the amount of state income tax deduction, review **Table A1 on page 16** in this publication.

Let's look at an example of how to use the state income tax Table A1.

Let's assume you live in the state of California and your taxable income is $125,000. Your state income tax deduction that will be used to calculate your EFC would be $7,500 **($125,000 X 6% = $7,500)**.

If you have a student that had earned an income of $3,000 while working in California, their state income tax deduction for EFC calculation would be $150.00 **($3,000 X 5% = $150)**.

STEP THREE: Size of Family Very Important

The Federal Methodology Formula will give a deduction based on the size of the family. The more family members you have living in your household, the larger the deduction. Refer to **Table A3** in this publication. **(Figures in this table could vary from year to year.)**

Let's look at a few examples: Let's assume you have a family size of 4 with 1 student in college. Your deduction against total available income when calculating your EFC would be $27,440. If you have a family size of 2, your deduction would be $17,840. If you had a family size of 5 with three in college, your deduction would be $26,290.

STEP FOUR: Employment Expense Allowance

The Federal Methodology Formula takes into consideration the cost of one (single parent) or two parents working. If only one parent **(married)** is employed, you **CANNOT** take the employment expense allowance.

If a single parent or both parents are employed, the Federal Methodology Formula will calculate the employment expense allowance by taking the **lowest income** of the parents or single parent X 35%, but this allowance cannot be more than $4,000.

For example: If the Mother earned $75,000 a year and the Father made $35,000, the family would be able to deduct a maximum of $4,000 **($35,000 X 35% = $12,250 {deduction cannot exceed $4,000}).** If Father earned $75,000 and the Mother earned $9,500, the family would be able to take a maximum employment expense allowance of $3,325 **($9,500 X 35% = $3,325).**

STEP FIVE: Asset Protection Allowance

When it comes to how assets are counted in the financial aid formula, parents get an allowance (called the Asset Protection Allowance). Students however **DO NOT** get an Asset Protection Allowance, and any of their exposed assets are assessed at a flat 20% assessment rate.

The Asset Protection Allowance is based on the age of the **oldest parent** in the household. The older the parent, the larger the protection allowance. Refer to **Table A7** in this publication. **(Figures in this table could vary from year to year.)**

Let's look at what assets are assessed and what assets are not. The list below will cover the assets that **will be included** in calculating the EFC of the family.

Investments include real estate **(not the home you live in)**, trust funds, UGMA and UTMA accounts, money market funds, mutual funds, certificates of deposit, stocks, stock options, bonds, other securities, installment and land sale contracts **(including mortgages held)**, commodities, etc.

Investments also include qualified educational benefits or education savings accounts such as Coverdell Savings Accounts, 529 College Savings Plans and the **refund value** of 529 Prepaid Tuition Plans. *For a student who does not report parental information, the accounts owned by the student (and the student's spouse) are reported as the student's assets on the FAFSA.* For a student who must report parental information, the accounts are reported as parental investments, **including all accounts owned by the student and all accounts owned by the parents for any member of the household in the FAFSA application.**

Now let's look at assets that are **NOT** included in the Federal Methodology Formula.

- **Investments don't include:** equity value in your home, cash value of life insurance, retirement plans (401[k] plans, pension funds, annuities, non-education IRAs, etc.)
- **Business value** - the value of a small business that you (your spouse and/or your parents/relatives) own and control and that has **100 or fewer full-time or full-time equivalent employees.**
- **Investment farm value** - the value of a family farm that you **(your spouse and/or your parents)** live on and operate.

16

Important Note: *Investment value means the current balance or market value of an investment as of today (date of completing the FAFSA). Investment debt means only those debts that are related to the investment.* The FAFSA wants to know the net worth of your investments **(value of investment <u>minus</u> debt on the assets = Net Worth).**

Here is an example: Let's assume you had an asset that was worth $100,000 and you used the asset as collateral to buy a car for $25,000. The value that you would put on the FAFSA would be $75,000 **($100,000 - $25,000 = $75,000).**

Very Important Note: *Over the years, high school parents have been told that having high* <u>**ASSETS**</u> *will disqualify the student from receiving financial aid, especially if the assets are in the student's name.* **This is very misleading.** *Most students will attend a state-supported college or university where assets will play a* <u>**very small role**</u> *in determining federal financial aid based on* <u>**NEED**</u>. *Even if you qualify for Need-Based financial aid it will likely come in the form of a Subsidized Stafford Loan, instead of an Unsubsidized Stafford Loan or* **PLUS Loan** *(Parent Loan). Before shifting any assets, talk to your CPA or a college advisor.*

Here is the reason we make this statement.

As we have already reviewed, parents receive an Asset Protection Allowance based on the age of the older parent in the family. A parent who is married (age 45) for example would have an Asset Protection Allowance of over $6,300 **(2015).**

Therefore, if you have assessable assets under $6,300 **(outside of a Pension Plan or IRA)** the federal financial aid formula will <u>**NOT**</u> count these assets against the student's financial aid eligibility. However, if the parents' assets are above this limit, the financial aid formula will assess the overage at a 5.65% rate.

For Example: Let's say you have $20,000 sitting in a mutual fund. The financial aid formula would subtract $6,300 from the $20,000, which would leave $13,700 that would be used to calculate the student's aid eligibility. The reduction in student financial aid would be approximately $774 **($13,700 x .0565 = $774).**

However, If you are a high-income earner, you most likely will not qualify for **Need Based** financial aid if your student attends an in-state, publicly-supported college or university. Therefore, shifting assets into a student's name could be an **ADVANTAGE** to the family because of the student's lower tax bracket. *Before moving assets into a student's name, make sure you talk to your CPA in regards to the Kiddie Tax Rules.*

Remember, in most situations, assets are not the **MOST** important factor that will disqualify the student from receiving financial aid. The most important factor is **INCOME**.
If a student has a large amount of assets in their name, calculate the Family's Expected Contribution **(EFC)** using **INCOME** of the parents and student **FIRST**. If your EFC, **(from income**

only) is within $5,000 of the **Total Cost of Attending** a public or private college, shifting assets will have little impact on financial aid

VERY IMPORTANT NOTE DEALING WITH SHIFTING ASSETS:

Financial aid comes in several forms:

- **Scholarships/Grants (Based on need and merit)**
- **Student Loans**
- **Work-Study**
- **Parent Loans**

According to the College Board, most financial aid is given out in the form of **LOANS**. Also remember, the **Financial Aid Officer (FAO)** at the college is the **ONLY** individual who will **determine how much financial aid is offered and in WHAT FORM**. Just because you shift assets and decrease your Expected Family Contribution there is **NO** assurance the Financial Aid Officer will provide assistance in the form of **FREE MONEY (scholarships/grants)**. They may simply offer more loans.

When considering asset shifting you need to determine if the maneuver **will increase the amount of FREE MONEY (scholarships/grants) or simply increase the amount you can borrow. This is very important!**

Two other things to consider when evaluating the impact of shifting assets are the **COSTS** of selling the assets and the impact on your **TAXES. The costs and taxes may be more than the potential increase in financial aid. This is also very important!**

Now let's look at a few abbreviations and definitions you need to know before calculating the **Total Expected Family Contribution.**

DEFINITIONS YOU NEED TO KNOW

TI - stands for Total Income. **TI** for the student and parents is income from all sources **(e.g., earned, unearned, untaxed, and income from asset conversion).**

AI - stands for Adjusted Income. **AI** is income from all sources **MINUS** all allowances and deductions **(e.g., Income Protection Allowance, Employment Expense Allowance, Asset Conversion Allowance, and all taxes paid).**

Note: Students and parents have different **AI amounts.** Students have a **FLAT** Income Protection Allowance of $6,400 **(2016-2017 school year)** *MINUS* any taxes paid X 50%. The student's assets are assessed at a **FLAT** 20% of the value of the asset and the student **DOES NOT** get an Asset Protection Allowance. The dependent student also **DOES NOT** get an Employment Expense Allowance.

16

AAI - stands for Adjusted Available Income. **AAI** is the total available income from the student and parents after **SUBTRACTING** present income levels for the parents and student and the **FLAT** asset assessment rate for the student.

TEFC - stands for Total Expected Family Contribution. **TEFC** is the total of the student and parents' contributions toward college expenses. The **TEFC** is also called the Expected Family Contribution, better known as the family's **EFC**.

On the next few pages, you will find worksheets you can use to calculate the Expected Family Contribution. You will also find tables you will use in calculating the EFC for your family. **(Make several copies of the worksheets and tables.)** By using these tables and worksheets you can play *"what if" games* to see what happens when you adjust certain financial information. Consult with your college advisor or CPA to see if your adjustments can be incorporated.

IMPORTANT: figures in these tables can vary from one year to the next. **DO YOUR HOMEWORK!**

Calculating Parents' Contribution - PARENTS' INCOME IN 2015

1. Parents' Adjusted Gross Income - If negative, enter zero. _____
2. Untaxed income and benefits (401-K, IRA, 403-B, etc.) _____

3. TOTAL INCOME (Add lines 1 and 2. This may be a negative number) _____

ALLOWANCE AGAINST PARENTS' INCOME
4. 2015 income tax paid (IRS form 1040, 1040A, or 1040EZ). If negative, enter zero._____
5. State and other tax allowance (Table A1). If negative, enter zero.)_____
6. Parent 1 Social Security tax allowance (Table A2) _____
7. Parent 2 Social Security tax allowance (Table A2) _____
8. Income protection allowance (Table A3) _____
9. Employment expense allowance:
• Two working parents: 35% of the lesser of the earned incomes, or $4,000, whichever is less
• One-parent families: 35% of earned income, or $4,000, whichever is less
• Two-parent families, one working parent: enter zero_____

10. TOTAL ALLOWANCES _____
11. AVAILABLE INCOME (AI) - Total income from line 3 **(Minus)** Total allowances from line 10) – may be a negative number_____
ASSET CONVERSION TO INCOME

12. Cash, savings, and checking_____
13. Net worth of investments* - If negative, enter zero_____
14. Net worth of business and/or investment farm -** If negative, enter zero_____
15. Adjusted net worth of business/farm (Calculate using Table A4.) _____
16. Net worth (sum of lines 12, 13, and 14) _____
17. Education savings and asset protection allowance (Table A7) _____
18. Discretionary net worth (line 16 minus line 17) _____

19. CONTRIBUTION FROM ASSETS - Discretionary net worth X .12 (Refer to Table A8) If negative, enter zero_____

PARENTS' CONTRIBUTION

20. AVAILABLE INCOME (AI) (from line 11) _____
21. CONTRIBUTION FROM ASSETS (from line 19) _____
22. Adjusted Available Income (AAI) (Add lines 20 and 21) _____
23. Total parents' contribution from AAI (Calculate using Table A9.) _____
24. Number of students in household in college in 2016-2017 (Exclude parents) _____
25. PARENTS' CONTRIBUTION - (divide line 23 by line 24 - if negative, enter zero_____

***Do *not* include the family's home ** Do not include business value if employing less than 100 employees or Family Farm**

CALCULATING A STUDENT'S CONTRIBUTION - STUDENT'S INCOME IN 2015

26. Adjusted Gross Income - If negative, enter zero_____
27. Untaxed income and benefits, (401-K, IRA, 403-B, etc.) _____

28. TOTAL INCOME (add lines 26 and 27) May be a negative number_____

ALLOWANCES AGAINST STUDENT INCOME

29. 2015 U.S. income tax paid (IRS form 1040, 1040A, or 1040EZ)._____
30. State and other tax allowance (Table A1). If negative, enter zero_____
31. Social Security tax allowance (Table A2) _____

32. TOTAL ALLOWANCES (Add lines 29, 30, and 31+ 6,400) (refer to Table A5) _____

STUDENT'S CONTRIBUTION FROM INCOME

33. Total income (from line 28) _____
34. Total allowances (from line 32) _____
35. Available income (AI) (subtract line 28 and 34) _____
36. STUDENT'S CONTRIBUTION FROM AI (multiple line 35 X .50) if negative, enter zero _____.

STUDENT'S CONTRIBUTION FROM ASSETS

37. Cash, savings & checking_____

38. Net worth of investments* - If negative, enter zero_____

39. Net worth of business and/or investment farm** - If negative, enter zero_____

40. Net worth (add lines 37, 38, and 39) _____

41. STUDENT'S CONTRIBUTION FROM ASSETS (multiple line 40 X .20) (refer to Table A6) _____

CALCULATING TOTAL EXPECTED FAMILY CONTRIBUTION (EFC) - TOTAL EXPECTED FAMILY CONTRIBUTION

42. PARENTS' CONTRIBUTION (from line 25) _____

43. STUDENT'S CONTRIBUTION FROM AI (from line 36) _____

44. STUDENT'S CONTRIBUTION FROM ASSETS (from line 41) _____

45. TOTAL EXPECTED FAMILY CONTRIBUTION (EFC) (add lines 42, 43, and 44) - If negative, enter zero_____

* **(# 38) Do *not* include the family's home equity value.**

** **(# 39) Do not include business value if employing less than 100 employees or Family Farm.**

Table A1: State and Other Tax Allowances

State	Parents of dependents and independents with dependents other than a spouse		Dependents and independents without dependents other than a spouse
	Percent of total income		
	Under $15,000	$15,000 & Up	All (%)
Alabama	3	2	2
Alaska	2	1	0
Arizona	4	3	2
Arkansas	4	3	3
California	7	6	5
Colorado	4	3	3
Connecticut	8	7	5
Delaware	5	4	3
District of Columbia	7	6	5
Florida	3	2	1
Georgia	5	4	3
Hawaii	5	4	4
Idaho	5	4	3
Illinois	6	5	3
Indiana	4	3	3
Iowa	5	4	3
Kansas	5	4	3
Kentucky	5	4	4
Louisiana	3	2	2
Maine	6	5	4
Maryland	8	7	5
Massachusetts	6	5	4
Michigan	4	3	3
Minnesota	6	5	4
Mississippi	3	2	2
Missouri	4	3	3
Montana	4	3	3
Nebraska	5	4	3
Nevada	2	1	1
New Hampshire	5	4	1
New Jersey	9	8	4
New Mexico	3	2	2
New York	9	8	6
North Carolina	5	4	4
North Dakota	2	1	1
Ohio	5	4	3
Oklahoma	3	2	2
Oregon	7	6	5
Pennsylvania	5	4	3
Rhode Island	7	6	3
South Carolina	4	3	3
South Dakota	2	1	1
Tennessee	2	1	1
Texas	3	2	1
Utah	5	4	3
Vermont	6	5	3
Virginia	6	5	4
Washington	3	2	1
West Virginia	3	2	2
Wisconsin	7	6	4
Wyoming	1	0	1
Other	2	1	1

Table A2: Social Security Tax

Social Security taxes are assessed at 7.65% of earned income. The following table will show you how to calculate your social security tax. Keep in mind these income figures could be adjusted each year.

16

- 6.2% on earned income up to $118,500
- 1.45% on **ALL INCOME**
- **Total 7.65%**

Example: If you earned $80,000, your social security tax is - $6,120 (**$80,000 X 7.65% = $6,120**). If you earned $150,000 your social security tax is - $9,522 (**$118,500 X 7.65% = $9,065 + {$150,000 - $118,500 = $31,500 X 1.45% = $457} = $9,522**)

Important Note: *If you invest into a 401-K, you don't pay federal or state income taxes for your contribution. However, the federal government **DOES** withhold social security taxes. When calculating your social security tax deduction, include the social security taxes paid on 401-K contributions.*

Example: If your **taxable income** was $80,000 and you contributed $3,000 into a 401-K plan, calculate your social security tax on the $3,000 401-K contribution (**$80,000 X 7.65% = $6,120 + $3,000 401-K contribution X 7.65% = $230 = $6,350**).

Table A3: Income Protection Allowance

The Federal Methodology Formula will give a deduction based on the size of the family. The more family members you have living in your household, the larger the deduction. The table below will outline the amount of deductions you could receive.

Family size	Parents of dependent students Number in college				
	1	2	3	4	5
2	$17,840	$14,790			
3	$22,220	$19,180	$16,130		
4	$27,440	$ 24,390	$21,350	$18,300	
5	$32,380	$ 29,320	$ 26,290	$23,240	$20,200
6	$37,870	$ 34,820	$ 31,780	$28,730	$25,690

If you have more than six family members, add **$4,270** for each additional family member. If you have more than 5 students in college at a time, subtract **$3,040** for each additional student.

Let's look at a few examples: Let's assume you have a family size of 4 with 1 student in college. Your deduction against total available income with calculating your EFC would be $27,440. If you have a family size of 2, your deduction would be $17,840. If you had a family size of 5 with three in college, your deduction would be $26,290.

Table A4: Business/Farm Net Worth Adjustment

If the net worth is	Then the adjusted business or farm Net worth is
Less than $1	$0
$1 to $125,000	40% of net worth of business/farm
$125,001 to $380,000	$50,000 + 50% of net worth over $125,000
$380,001 to $635,000	$177,500 +60% of net worth over $380,000
$635,001 or more	$330,500 + 100% of net worth over $635,000

IMPORTANT NOTE: If you own a business or farm, and you employ **LESS** than 100 employees, **DO NOT** use this table. The value of the business or farm would not be counted as an available asset.

Table A5: Student's Income Protection Allowance

Student Income	Contribution
0 to $6,400	$0
$6,401 or more	50% minus any taxes paid

Table A6: Student's Asset Conversation

Total Accessable Assets	Contribution
$1 or more	20% of accessable assets

Example: If the student has $10,000 outside of a pension plan **(e.g., UGMA or UTMA)** their income contribution from the asset is $2,000 each year based on the account value from year to year (**$10,000 X 20% = $2,000**).

Table A7: Saving and Asset Allowances

PARENTS OF DEPENDENT STUDENTS

If the age of the older parent is	And they are	
	Married	Single
	Then the education savings and asset protection allowance is	
25 or less	0	0
26	400	200
27	700	400
28	1,100	600
29	1,500	900
30	1,900	1,100
31	2,200	1,300
32	2,600	1,500
33	3,000	1,700
34	3,400	1,900
35	3,700	2,100
36	4,100	2,300
37	4,500	2,600
38	4,900	2,800
39	5,200	3,000
40	5,600	3,200
41	5,700	3,300
42	5,900	3,400
43	6,000	3,500
44	6,100	3,500
45	6,300	3,600
46	6,400	3,700
47	6,600	3,800
48	6,800	3,900
49	6,900	4,000
50	7,100	4,000
51	7,300	4,100
52	7,500	4,200
53	7,700	4,300
54	7,900	4,400
55	8,100	4,600
56	8,300	4,700
57	8,500	4,800
58	8,800	4,900
59	9,000	5,000
60	9,300	5,100
61	9,500	5,300
62	9,800	5,400
63	10,100	5,500
64	10,400	5,700
65 or older	10,700	5,800

Table A8: Parents Income Conversion From Assets

Value of Asset	Conversion to Income
$1 and over	12% X value of asset <u>minus</u> asset protection allowance

Example: Any assessable asset must be converted to income. If the parents have $20,000 in an investment that is outside of a retirement account, they must convert the asset into income. To do this, **SUBTRACT** the Asset Protection Allowance **(based on the age of the oldest parent Table A7)** from the present value of the investment. Then take the remaining value times 12%.

Here is how it will look when dealing with a parent that is age 48: **($20,000 - $6,800 {from table A7} = $13,200 X 12% = $1,584).**

The $1,584 is then added to the parents' Available Income **(AI)**. If in this case the parents' Available Income from all earnings was $40,000, you would add the **Income Conversion From Assets** to this value (i.e. $40,000 + $1,584 = $41,584), which will give you the parents' Adjusted Available Income **(AAI)**. If you look at **Table A9**, you will see this family is in the 47% assessment rate **(their AAI is over $32,200)**. Based on this table the $13,200 in assets will increase the parents' EFC by **$745 (1,584 X 47% = $745)**.

You may hear from college advisors **"Take your total assessible asset minus your asset protection allowance X 5.65% to come up with the amount that must be used to pay for college expenses."** Based on the above example here is how this would look:

$20,000 - $6,800 = $13,200 X 5.65% = $746. As you will notice this is only **$1 more** than the **ACTUAL** assessment from the calculation in the Federal Methodology calculation.

Table A9: Parents' Expected Contribution

The table below is used to calculate the **Parents' Expected Contribution**. AAI stands for Adjusted Available Income. AAI is the combination of **ALL** available income. The parents' contribution for a dependent student is computed according to the following schedule:

If AAI is:	Then the contribution is:
Less than $3,409	**-$750**
$3,409 to $15,900	**22% of AAI**
$15,901 to $20,000	**$3,498 + 25% of AAI over $15,900**
$20,001 to $24,100	**$4,523 + 29% of AAI over $20,000**
$24,101 to $28,200	**$5,712 + 34% of AAI over $24,100**
$28,201 to $32,200	**$7,106 + 40% of AAI over $28,200**
$32,201 or more	**$8,706 + 47% of AAI over $32,200**

As I have mentioned before, understanding how your EFC is calculated may help you pay for college. You need to know how the figures you report on the FAFSA are used and how you can benefit by rearranging your income and assets.

When it comes to paying for college, calculating your Expected Family Contribution **(EFC)** is the **FIRST** step in solving the problem of how to pay for college. Knowing approximately what the colleges will expect you to pay **BEFORE** and **DURING** your student stay in college is **VERY** important.

16

On the next few pages, I will give you an example of calculating the EFC by using the tables and worksheets that are in this publication.

Sample of Calculating Your Expected Family Contribution

The Norm Family:

The Norm Family's Background

The Norm Family lives in the state of New York. Mr. and Mrs. Norm both work and have two children, Bob and Susan. Bob is looking at attending a public or private college in the fall of 2016. Bob **(the student)** earns approximately $3,900 in income during the year working at a local sporting goods store and normally has a balance of $500 in his checking account monthly. The public college costs $24,000, and the private college costs $48,000 a year.

> The worst mistake on the financial aid forms is to input the wrong Social Security number. Double check the numbers for your student and yourself. *– Coach Ryan*

Mr. Norm earns $85,000 a year, and Mrs. Norm earns $48,000. Mr. Norm is 49 years old. Mr. and Mrs. Norm contribute a total of $8,000 between themselves into their 401-K ($4,000 each). Mr. and Mrs. Norm have saved a total of $60,000 in a 529 Savings Plan ($30,000 for each child) to help pay for college expenses. The Norm family has a balance in checking and savings monthly of about $6,300.

Calculation of the Norm's EFC can be found on the next few pages

CALCULATING PARENTS' CONTRIBUTION for the Norm Family

PARENTS' INCOME IN 2015

1. Parents' Adjusted Gross Income - If negative, enter zero - **$133,000**
2. Untaxed income and benefits: (401-K, IRA, etc.) - **$8,000 (401-K contributions - $4,000 each)**

3. TOTAL INCOME (add lines 1 and 2) May be a negative number - **$141,000** (taxed and untaxed income)

ALLOWANCE AGAINST PARENTS' INCOME

4. 2015 income tax paid (IRS form 1040, 1040A, or 1040EZ). If negative, enter zero - **$18,800**
5. State and other tax allowance **(Table A1)** if negative, enter zero. - **$10,640** **(8% of $133,000)**
6. Father's/stepfather's Social Security tax allowance **(Table A2)** - **$6,809** (includes 401-K contributions
7. Mother's/stepmother's Social Security tax allowance **(Table A2)** - **$3,978** (include 401-K contributions
8. Income protection allowance **(Table A3)** - **$27,440** **(family of 4 with one in college)**
9. Employment expense allowance: • Two working parents: 35% of the lesser of the earned incomes, or $4,000, whichever is less • One-parent families: 35% of earned income, or $4,000, whichever is less • Two-parent families, one working parent: enter zero - **$4,000** **(35% of $40,000 = $14,000 {$4,000 max}**

10. TOTAL ALLOWANCES - $71,667

AVAILABLE INCOME

11. AVAILABLE INCOME (AI) - Total income from line 3 **(Minus)** Total allowances from line 10) – may be a negative number - **$69,333** ($141,000 total income - $71,667 total allowances)

ASSET CONVERSION TO INCOME

12. Cash, savings, and checking - **$6,300** **(checking and savings)**
13. Net worth of investments* - If negative, enter zero - **$60,000** **(529 Savings Accounts)**
14. Net worth of business and/or investment farm -** If negative, enter zero - **$0**
15. Adjusted net worth of business/farm (Calculate using Table A4.) - **$0**
16. Net worth (sum of lines 12, 13, and 14) - **$66,300**
17. Education savings and asset protection allowance (Table A7) - **$6,900**
18. Discretionary net worth (line 16 minus line 17) - **$59,400**

19. CONTRIBUTION FROM ASSETS - Discretionary net worth X .12 (Refer to Table A8) If negative, enter zero - **$7,128** ($59,400 discretionary net worth X 12%)

PARENTS' CONTRIBUTION

20. AVAILABLE INCOME (AI) (from line 11) - **$69,333**
21. CONTRIBUTION FROM ASSETS (from line 19) - **$7,128**
22. Adjusted Available Income (AAI) (Add lines 20 and 21) May be a negative number - **$76,461**

23. Total parents' contribution from AAI (Calculate using Table A9.) - **$29,508**
 ($8,706 on first $32,201 plus 47% on the remaining $44,260 = $20,802)
24. Number of students in household in college in 2016-2017 (Exclude parents) - **1**
25. PARENTS' CONTRIBUTION - (divide line 23 by line 24 - if negative, enter zero - **$29,508**
($29,508 divided by 1) = $29,508 PARENTS EFC

16

*Do *not* include the family's home ** Do not include business value if employing less than 100
employees or Family Farm*

CALCULATING Bob's STUDENT CONTRIBUTION

STUDENT'S INCOME IN 2015

26. Adjusted Gross Income - If negative, enter zero - **$3,900**
27. Untaxed income and benefits: Total from FAFSA (401-K, IRA, etc.) - **$0**

28. TOTAL INCOME (Add lines 26 and 27) May be a negative number - **$3,900**

ALLOWANCES AGAINST STUDENT INCOME

29. 2015 U.S. income tax paid (IRS form 1040, 1040A, or 1040EZ). If negative, enter zero - **$0**
 (The student receives a standard deduction of $6,300 in 2015)
30. State and other tax allowance (Table A1) if negative, enter zero - **$351 (9% state tax)**
31. Social Security tax allowance (Table A2) - **$298 (7.65% X $3,900)**

32. TOTAL ALLOWANCES (Add lines 29, 30, and 31+ 6,400) (refer to Table A5) - **$13,349**

STUDENT'S CONTRIBUTION FROM INCOME

33. Total income (from line 28) - **$3,900**
34. Total allowances (from line 32) - **$13,349**
35. Available income (AI) (subtract line 28 and 34) - **$0**

36. STUDENT'S CONTRIBUTION FROM AI (multiple lines 35 X .50). If negative, enter zero - **$0.**

STUDENT'S CONTRIBUTION FROM ASSETS

37. Cash, savings & checking - **$500**
38. Net worth of investments* - If negative, enter zero - **$0**
39. Net worth of business and/or investment farm** - If negative, enter zero - **$0**
40. Net worth (add lines 37, 38, and 39) - **$500**

41. STUDENT'S CONTRIBUTION FROM ASSETS (multiple line 40 X .20) (refer to Table A6) - **$100**

CALCULATING TOTAL EXPECTED FAMILY CONTRIBUTION (EFC)

TOTAL EXPECTED FAMILY CONTRIBUTION

42. PARENTS' CONTRIBUTION (from line 25) - **$29,508**
43. STUDENT'S CONTRIBUTION FROM AI (from line 36) - **$0**
44. STUDENT'S CONTRIBUTION FROM ASSETS (from line 41) - **$100**
45. TOTAL EXPECTED FAMILY CONTRIBUTION (EFC) (add lines 42, 43, and 44) - If negative, enter zero - **$29,608**

*   Do *not* include the family's home
** Do not include business value if employing less than 100 employees or Family Farm

SUMMARY

The Norm Family's Total Expected Family Contribution is as follows:

Mr. and Mrs. Norm -	$29,508
Bob Norm -	$100
Total Family EFC	$29,608

Public College Breakdown:

The total cost of attending the public college is:	$24,000
Norms' Expected Family Contribution (EFC) is:	- 29,608
Total Need:	$ 0

Since the Norms' EFC is <u>larger</u> than the cost of the public education, Bob will **NOT** qualify for any **NEED-BASED AID**. Bob could qualify for $5,500 in Unsubsidized Stafford Loans during his first year in college, and his parents could qualify for a **PLUS** (Parent Loan for Undergraduate Student) up to the total cost of attending <u>minus</u> any student aid the student may receive.

Private College Breakdown:

The total cost of attending the private college is:	$48,000
Norms' Total Expected Family Contribution is (EFC):	- 29,608
Total Need:	$ 18,392

Since the Norm family's EFC is <u>lower</u> than the cost of the private college, Bob will qualify for **NEED-BASED AID**. How the private college packages their financial aid offer is totally up to the Financial Aid Officer at the college.

- Bob could qualify for a $3,500 Subsidized and an additional $2,000 in Unsubsidized Stafford Loan.
- He could qualify for $12,892 in Need-Based scholarships or grants or Federal Work-Study.

- His parents could qualify for a PLUS (Parent Loan for Undergraduate Student) up to the total cost of attendance (COA) __minus__ any student aid the student may receive.
- Since many private colleges give out merit-based scholarships, Bob could also receive this money based on his academic success as well to help offset the cost based on his academic success.

Because the Norm family's income is under $160,000 they should qualify for the American Opportunity Tax Credit of $2,500 IF they pay at least $4,000 toward qualified expenses. This would be claimed on their tax return.

Take the time to run your EFC numbers, talk to each college and understand what college funding options will be available to your son or daughter so that there are NO surprises after a final college decision has been made.

As a BONUS: Here are 12 of the Most Commonly asked Questions about Financial Aid

1. *I probably don't qualify for financial aid. Should I apply for aid anyway?*

   Yes. Many families mistakenly think they will not qualify for financial aid. By not filling out the paperwork, these families prevent themselves from receiving the aid they are eligible to receive. Please remember, financial aid comes in two forms: free money (scholarships and grants) and debt or earned money (loans and work-study). Unsubsidized Stafford Loans are available to every student and parents can apply for PLUS Loans. The FAFSA form is free, so you should always complete it as a backup plan.

2. *Do I have to reapply for financial aid every year?*

   Yes. Colleges and Universities require a student to apply for financial aid every year. If your financial circumstances change, you may get more or less aid. **Note**: your eligibility for financial aid may change significantly, especially if you have a different number of family members in college at the same time. Renewal of your financial aid package also depends on the student making satisfactory academic progress towards a degree, such as earning a minimum number of credits and achieving a minimum GPA.

3. *How do I apply for a Grant and other types of Federal need-based aid?*

   Submit a FAFSA or the CSS Profile. To indicate interest in student employment, student loans, and parent loans, you should check the appropriate boxes. Checking these boxes does not commit you to accepting these types of aid. You will have the opportunity to accept or decline each part of your aid package later when you receive your official Award Letter from your college. Leaving these boxes unchecked will not increase the amount of grants you receive.

4. *Are my parents responsible for my educational loans?*

NO. But parents are responsible for the Federal PLUS loans they take out in their own name. The exception is IF parents co-sign on any of a student's private college loans. In general, you (student) and you alone are responsible for repaying your educational loans. On the other hand, if your parents (or grandparents) want to help pay off your loan(s), you can have your billing statements sent to their address. Likewise, if your lender or loan company provides an electronic payment service where the monthly payments are automatically deducted from a bank account, your parents can agree to have the payments deducted from their account. But your parents are under no obligation to repay your individual college loans. If they forget to pay the bill on time or decide to cancel the electronic payment agreement, you will be held responsible for the late payments, not them.

5. *Why is the family contribution listed on the Student Aid Report (SAR) different from the family contribution expected by the university?*

The federal formula for computing the expected family contribution (EFC) can be different from those used by a number of private universities. In particular, the federal formula does not consider home equity as part of the assets, yet some colleges will take home equity into consideration when determining how much of their institutional funds they are willing to give a student.

6. *If I take a leave of absence from college, do I have to start repaying my loans?*

Not immediately. The subsidized Stafford loan has a grace period of 6 months and the Perkins loan has a grace period of 9 months before the student must begin repaying the loan. When you take a leave of absence, you will not have to repay your loan until the grace period is used up. If you use up the grace period, however, when you graduate you will have to begin repaying your loan immediately. It is possible to request an extension to the grace period, but this must be done before the grace period is used up. If your grace period has run out in the middle of your leave of absence, you will have to start making payments on your student loans.

7. *I received an outside scholarship. Should I report it to the financial aid office?*

Yes. If you are receiving any outside scholarships from any sources, you are expected to report this dollar amount to the financial aid office at your university. Unfortunately, it is possible the university will adjust your financial aid package down to compensate for these funds. At some universities, outside scholarships are applied first to reduce institutional aid that a student receives (grants and scholarships) and in other cases they will thankfully be used to reduce the amount of student loans.

8. *Are Federal Work-Study earnings taxable?*

> **Yes,** the money earned from Federal Work-Study is generally subject to federal and state income tax, but exempt from FICA taxes (provided you are enrolled full time and work less than half-time). The student should be careful to report amounts based on the calendar year, not the school year. Also, the money earned from Work-Study does not negatively affect future financial aid eligibility.

9. *How do I file the FAFSA financial aid form?*

> You may choose any of these three methods to file a Free Application for Federal Student Aid (FAFSA): (1) Apply online at http://www.fafsa.ed.gov (recommended), (2) or Complete a PDF FAFSA (which must be mailed for processing), (3) or request a paper FAFSA by calling the Federal Student Aid Information Center at 1-800-4-FED-AID or (1-800-433-3243 FREE) or 1-319-337-5665. If you are hearing impaired, please contact the TTY line at 1-800-730-8913 for FREE.

10. *My parents are separated or divorced. Which parent is responsible for filling out the FAFSA? What about the CSS Profile?*

> If your parents are separated or divorced, the "custodial parent" is responsible for filling out the **FAFSA**. The custodial parent is the parent with whom you lived the most during the past 12 months. (Note that this is not necessarily the same as the parent who has legal custody or the parent who claims the student on their tax return.) If you did not live with one parent more than the other, the parent who provided you with the most financial support during the past twelve months should fill out the FAFSA. If you have not received any support from either parent during the past 12 months, use the most recent calendar year tax return for which you received some support from a parent.

> **PLEASE NOTE:** Any child support and/or alimony received from the non-custodial parent must be included on the FAFSA. When it comes to the **CSS Profile**, financial details (income and assets) from **both** parents (**and step-parents if remarried**) need to be listed.

11. *My parents are divorced, and the parent I'm living with has remarried. Does my step-parent have to report his or her income and assets on the FAFSA? What about the CSS Profile?*

> **Yes,** provided that the parent with whom you are living (your custodial parent) is the one filling out the FAFSA. If the step-parent is married to your custodial parent at the time you will out the FAFSA, they must report their income and assets, even if they weren't married to them for the entire previous year.

When it comes to the **CSS Profile**, financial details (income and assets) from both parents and step-parents need to be listed. In other words, the student could end up having financial details from 2 parents and 2 step-parents (4 total) taken into consideration when the college calculates their Expected Family Contribution (EFC) when using the Institutional Methodology.

12. *My custodial parent remarried and signed a prenuptial agreement that absolves the step-parent from financial responsibility for my education. Why does my step-parent have to provide financial information on the FAFSA?*

Prenuptial agreements are ignored by the federal need analysis process. After all, two individuals (parent and step-parent) cannot make an agreement between them that is binding on a third party (the federal government). The federal government considers the step-parent a source of support regardless of any prenuptial agreements to the contrary. If a step-parent marries the parent, he or she is considered responsible for supporting the parent and child (ren), even if he or she is unwilling to do so.

If you have any questions or need additional help calculating your EFC, *please feel free to contact Dan or Ryan today!*

> Every family has an *Expected Family Contribution* (EFC). Knowing yours TODAY and dealing with the shock and awe that can paralyze any family is critical so that you can plan accordingly. Remember, there is often only one person who can reduce a high EFC amount, the student. How? By qualifying for scholarships! — *Coach Dan*

Remember to visit Coach Dan's website www.collegeandbeyondllc.com and Coach Ryan's website www.collegeaidformiddleclass.com to find additional resources on this important topic!

College Budget

"You are never a loser until you quit trying."   — Mike Ditka, NFL Player and Coach

Do you have a Game Plan for funding college?
If not…it could cost you thousands of extra dollars!

When it comes to the college process, there are Two BIG MISTAKES that we see many parents and students make. The first is when parents have NOT gotten around to working through their College Budget. We are going to help you with this in the next few pages of this Chapter. The second is when we meet with students and ask them three important questions:

1. Why do you want to go to college?
2. Where do you want to go to college, and why?
3. What career (vocation) are you looking to pursue, and why?

The lack of thought process is evident when we get answers from students such as; "I don't know", OR "Because that's where my friends are going to school", OR "I'll figure it out once I get to college". Simple answers like this not only show a terrible lack of planning, but will almost assuredly cost these families a minimum of $10,000 to $20,000 in added expense as they try to figure things out. **Students, use the terrific resources in Chapter 11 to plan your future!**

Why is it imperative for students and parents to plan ahead?

- The average cost of college has risen dramatically over the years, while the average income or savings for most families has not kept pace. According to the College Board, the average cost of tuition and fees for the 2015–2016 school year was $32,405 at private colleges, $9,410 for state residents at public colleges, and $23,893 for out-of-state residents attending public universities. (**Please note**: this DOES NOT include room and board, books, transportation and other miscellaneous expenses).
- Thirty years ago, many students could pay for a 4 year public college education with a job or a few low-cost loans. Unfortunately, it is not uncommon today for students to graduate from college with $30,000 to $40,000 of debt at a minimum. In fact, the current total National College Debt amount is over **$1.3 TRILLION** which isn't slowing down.
- The cost of college is now so high that many parents are paying out huge chunks of their own disposable income and savings, and often borrowing more to cover any shortfall.

Today is the day for YOU to Take Action and Complete these College Budget Worksheets and BUILD Your College Funding Game Plan.

College Budget Worksheet

1. Tax Credit	Data Required for the Calculator			
	Filing Singly		Filing Jointly	
Use this information to determine your tax credit category for the year before your student begins college:	Adjusted Gross Income	Tax Credit Eligibility	Adjusted Gross Income	Tax Credit Eligibility
a. Determine if you will file your taxes singly or jointly.	Less than $80,000	$2,500.00	Less than $160,000	$2,500
b. Look to the correct table and choose one of the three categories to represent your household income.	$80,000-$89,999.99	$1,500.00	$160,000-$179,999.99	$1,500
	Greater than or equal to $90,000	$0.00	Greater than or equal to $180,000	$0
Example: Married Couple w/AGI of $110,000				*$2,500*
Total Tax Credit:				

2. Consider Lifestyle Changes	Description	Amount	# of Times Per Year	Total
Consider your current cash flow, how much do you believe you could contribute to college cost directly - either from non-allocated income or lifestyle sacrifices?				
For Example:	*Eliminate Big Vacations next 4 yrs.*	$2,300.00	1	$2,300.00
*Eating out less				
*Reduced entertainment expense				
*Use of public transportation				
*Excess cash not redirected				

*Quit Smoking				
*Reallocate Vacation money				
*Eliminate lattes, energy drinks, lottery tickets, candy bars,				
Total Lifestyle Changes:				

3. Get a Second Job	Description	Amount	# of Times Per Year	Total
Would you be willing to help your child graduate college debt- free? How much can you increase your take home pay, on a monthly basis?				
Example:	**Yearly Bonus**	**$4,000.00**	1	**$4,000.00**
Total Second Job:				

4. Sell Your Unused Items	Description	Amount	# of Times Per Year	Total
Consider a yard sale, Craigslist, or eBay for those unused items. Please estimate how much you can sell.				
What you cannot sell, you can donate for a tax write-off that can free up cash.				
Example:	*Sell Old Clothes, Toys, Furniture*	**$500.00**	1	**$500.00**
Total of Unused Items:				

17

5. Is your Child Willing To Work In College?	Hourly Rate	# Hrs. per week	Avg. Weeks per Year	Monthly Total ($)
Working just 15 hrs. per week and earning $8 per hour, that is $120 per week or approximately $500 a month.				
If you multiply this by 8 months, you get $4,000 per year to help pay for college.				
Job Example: Part Time Job at Café	$8	15	40	$4,800.00
*caddying, personal trainer, tutoring, delivering newspapers, paid fellowships, entrepreneurship, temping, co-op				
Total Child Working Amount:				

6. Reduced Expenses	Description	Amount	# of Times Per Year	Monthly Total
Are there any expenses that will be reduced or eliminated because of your student leaving for college?				
Example:	*Reduced Weekly Grocery Bills*	$70.00	52	$3,640
*Reduced Grocery bills				
*Summer Camps				
*High School Tuition				
*Music Lesson or extracurricular expenses				
Total Reduced Expenses:				

7.Eliminate Financial Leaks	Description	Amount	# of Times Per Year	Total
Can you avoid unnecessary fees and preventable expenses? Can you eliminate any cost or fees before your child starts college?				
For Example:	*Increase Car Insurance Deductible*	**$200.00 Savings**	**1**	**$200.00**
*Refinance House to lower interest rate				
*Consolidate Debt to lower interest rate				
*Increase your auto insurance deductible				
*Increase your home insurance deductible				
*Shift after-tax dollars to child by annual gifting to lower tax rate				
*Eliminate Consumer Debt (credit card debt, etc.)				
*Mortgage Payments				
*Car Loans				
*Other loans				
Total Amount from Financial Leaks:				

8. Existing Savings	Description	Amount		Total
After your emergency fund, what savings can be used toward college cost?				
Example:	*529 Plan*	*$12,000.00*		*$12,000*
*529 Plan				
*Pre-paid tuition plan				
*UTMA account				
*Roth IRA (set up for college, do not use if for retirement)				

*IRA (set up for college, do not use if for retirement)				
Total from Existing Savings:				

9. Monthly Savings	Description	Amount	# of Times Per Year	Total
Does your employee match your 401(k)? Do you contribute above the match? Can you redirect this amount or any savings every month while your child is in college to help cover college cost?				
Example	*Stop my Excess Contribution above 401k match*	$800.00	12	$9,600.00
Yearly Amount from Monthly Savings:				

10. Other Miscellaneous Found Funds	Description	Amount	# of Times per Year	Total
Are there any other assets that are designated for college that have not been listed?				
Example:	Gift from Grandparents	$1,000.00	1	$1,000.00
*Inheritance				
*Gift from relative				
*Sale of property				
*Work bonus				

Total from Miscellaneous:				
Add up the TOTALS to determine your *College Budget*:				
Example				$40,540.00

17

Parent's, this dollar amount should represent the amount you can commit to helping your student pay for college. If the amount is $0, in other words there just isn't anything left to help pay for college then it is better to let your student know this now than to wait until it is too late! Take action and plan accordingly.

Please visit Coach Dan's website www.collegeandbeyondllc and Coach Ryan's website www.collegeaidformiddleclass.com if you need help with your college funding game plan!

Make sure you decide on your financial limits as a family and discuss those limits with your student. However, don't take a college off your list because of the price. Wait until you receive the financial aid awards to determine the final cost.
– Coach Ryan

For many families, budget is a nasty 4 letter word. Taking the time to understand where your family finances are today and identifying what, if anything can be committed toward paying for college is critical. Crunch the numbers today!
– Coach Dan

Paying for College

"Let me tell you what winning means...you're willing to go longer, work harder, give more than anyone else."
— Vince Lombardi, Football Coach

So you have been accepted to a college, and you have sent in your deposit. At this point, you are ready for the next critical step–figuring out how to pay for this 800-pound gorilla. If you followed all of the steps we outlined in Chapters 16 and 17, this should be a piece of cake. But let's say you just didn't get around to putting together your college funding game plan or the financial aid offers you received are less than you expected. You may be asking yourself "What are my options and what loans are available to help me to pay for college?"

First, you need to determine your true budget or how much out-of-pocket expense you will need to budget for over the years. The true college budget is the total yearly out-of-pocket cost for a student to attend college. To calculate your true budget, make sure you have your official financial aid award letter handy.

To understand the process, start with the **Cost of Attendance (COA)**. The COA is the estimated total cost for your child to attend college for one year. The COA may include tuition and fees, books, supplies, transportation, miscellaneous personal expenses, room and board fees. (Other costs may be included if you are a student with a dependent, or you are going to study abroad, or you need to cover additional fees for services offered to students with learning challenges).

Next, please subtract any grants and scholarships (free money) you might have received from the COA. If you will be taking out a Federal Stafford (Direct) Loan OR a Work-Study Job (called Self Help) offered by the school, please subtract these amounts from the COA as well. The amount that is left is your True Budget or out of pocket expense per year.

EXAMPLE:

Cost Of Attendance (COA):	**$49,032**
Grants/Scholarships:	($21,300)
Loan/Self Help	($9,500)
True Budget:	**$18,232**
Total Need Met ($21,300 + $9,500):	$30,800

In some cases, colleges will list a Federal Parent (PLUS) loan on the Award Letter as additional aid to help cover your True Budget. While a PLUS loan can be used to help pay for college, we would not consider this as aid from a college. You can read more about the pros and cons of the various student loans in the book *College Aid for Middle-Class America: Solutions to Paying Wholesale vs. Retail by Ryan Clark.*

Having worked with thousands of families, we have seen many different strategies families have implemented to pay the True Cost for college. Below are seven of the most common funding choices families choose:

Options for Paying for College:

Option #1 – Savings and Investments

This is by far the best college funding solution for a student if they are lucky enough to have parents who have been able to save through the years to pay for all or most of their college. But please be careful parents. The biggest downside to using your hard earned savings and investments to pay your child's college is that you are taking most of the financial risk. You are prepaying college with the hope they will graduate and find a job. Yes, this truly may be the best investment you ever made but make sure your son/daughter understands that funding his/her college education also comes with accountability, responsibility, and certain expectations.

What happens if something goes wrong along the way and your child does not graduate? The average 4 year graduation rate at 4 year public colleges in the United States hovers at around 37% (59% for 6 years). The key is to make sure your son/daughter understands the sacrifices you have been making for them. Hold them accountable for doing their part. Graduating from college in as short a period of time (with the only exception being a degree that takes longer) should be a non-negotiable expectation. Yes, college should be fun and filled with many great memories and friendships, but it also comes with an end goal of graduating and finding a job.

Option #2 – Monthly Tuition Payment Plans to pay for College: Cash Flow

Most colleges allow parents to make monthly payments to cover the remaining balance (True Budget). Essentially, colleges will divide your remaining balance equally using an installment plan lasting anywhere from ten to twelve months. Many colleges do not charge interest while you pay your balance using this short-term installment plan. The colleges deduct your payment amount from your checking or savings account each month. A few colleges also allow you to charge this on a credit card for an additional fee. However, many installment plans do have an enrollment fee (less than $100). For example, let's use $18,323 from above as the outstanding amount a student still owes. A college may allow a family to pay this amount over 12 months, or $1527 per month. The payments depend on what, if anything, you put down and when.

Make sure you ask about all costs and fees before starting a tuition installment plan. The installment plan is an excellent alternative to paying for college if you cannot afford a large lump sum payment at the beginning of the semester, but you must have the cash flow to cover the monthly payments.

Again, the only downside in using your disposable monthly cash flow to pay for college is the potential risk of having your student not finish college. We know what you are thinking: "Not my child, s/he will graduate." We absolutely hope you are right, but we have met with students who were bright, intelligent, and motivated when they entered college, but unfortunately made some bad decisions along the way, ended up extending their time in college or never graduated.

18

Option #3 – College Loans

There are two basic types of loans that a student and parent can take out to pay for college: **Federal and Private.** Let's talk about each of these.

Federal Loans:

- The Federal Direct (Stafford) Loan is available to a student who completes the FAFSA. This student loan does not require a credit score, job or co-signer. The maximum loan a student can take out in their freshman year is $5,500 (unless his/her parents are turned down for a PLUS loan). The current interest rate is 3.76%. (Loans are charged the current interest rate when taken out, so do your research.)

  Some families choose to have their student take out a federal student loan, even if they can pay for college, to put their child's "skin in the game". This strategy works great if mom and dad can help pay off some or all of those loans once the student graduates.

- The Federal Parent PLUS (Parent Loan for Undergraduate Student) Loan is offered to parents who complete the FAFSA. Parents qualify for this loan by completing an application (credit scores count) and the proceeds can be used to cover up to the total cost of a college or any remaining shortfall (gap) that exists. The current interest rate is 6.31%. (Loans are assessed the current each rate when taken out, some do your research.)

Private Loans:

The world of private college loans has changed over the years. Students and parents can take out loans from a variety of lenders with different interest rates and payment options. However, private loans do not come with the same advantages as federal college loans so proceed with caution!

Warning! Use private student and parent loans ONLY as a last resort. If private loans become part of your college funding solution, you may want to look at the www.simpletuition.com website to compare and contrast some of the lenders and loan details. Be careful, do your research and know exactly what you are taking out BEFORE you sign on the dotted line.

Warning! Remember that college loans can never be discharged through bankruptcy!

IF a family needs to take out loans to help pay for college, the best advice we can give you is that the student should start by taking out the Federal Direct (Stafford) Loan first. A Master Promissory Note will need to be signed by the student and s/he will need to complete loan counseling online at www.studentloans.gov.

Option #4 – Home Equity or Lines of Credit Loan

Home Equity Loans OR Lines Of Credit (HELOC) may have interest rates that are low compared to other college loans. In addition, a family may be able to qualify for a tax deduction (consult your tax preparer). Using an equity line of credit or home equity loan may be a good alternative to consider. This is especially true IF your college requires you to complete the CSS Profile and if they take home equity into consideration and add a portion of it to your Expected Family Contribution (EFC). If this is the case, then borrowing money from your home to help pay for college might be a great idea. Colleges who just use the FAFSA form do not use home equity (primary residence only) in their EFC calculation. By taking equity out of your home, you may be able to reduce your EFC at a Profile College BUT run the numbers and do your homework before you do anything. You must know the pros and cons of the decisions you make.

There is always another side of the coin with any option. For many, home equity is also considered a source of emergency funds that can be used in times of need. Sometimes small business owners use their home equity to cover month-to-month cash flow fluctuations. If you tap your equity to pay for college, this source of emergency funding is no longer available. In addition, because of the home mortgage crisis back in 2008, home values in your neighborhood may not have rebounded leading to less money to use for college or other emergency needs. Make sure you run the numbers BEFORE you do anything and always consult your advisers.

Option #5 – Downsize Your Lifestyle

Sometimes making minor changes in your lifestyle can have an enormous impact on how much you can save for college. Here are a few examples of where you can find money:

- A pack of cigarettes can cost anywhere from $5.00 to $11.00 depending on where you live. If we use $6.50 as an average cost, and you smoke a pack a day, this equals $45.50 per week or **$2,366** per year that could be used to help pay for college.

- How about if you cut back on spending that extra $5.00 per day on one of these miscellaneous items: coffee, energy drinks, snacks, lottery tickets, candy, etc. You could save **$1,820** per year to put toward college costs.
- Or maybe this year your family goes on a "staycation," instead of a weeklong extravagant vacation. The average family spends around **$2,200** per year on a vacation, so once again you have found some extra money.

In this example, just a few simple changes in your spending can add up to **$6,386** that could be put toward college. Wow, do this for four years and you have saved **$25,544!**

18

> # Take the time to complete your College Budget in Chapter 16 so that you can find additional money for college!

Option #6 – Have Student Work

This is one of our favorite college funding options–maybe we should have put this as option #1! Can your child work 20 hours a week in college and still get good grades? You had better believe it and there are studies that prove it! For example, *UPromise Inc.* found that students' "Working a limited number of hours (ex. 10 hours a week) at an on-campus job appears to have positive impacts on student performance". In addition, the *Journal of Student Financial Aid* found that students who work eleven to twenty hours per week had higher GPAs than students who did not work at all. These students seem to do a better job of staying focused on their task, have less time to party, and develop better time management skills.

If your child only works 20 hours per week at $8 per hour, s/he will earn **$160** per week. That equals around **$640** a month or **$7,680 a year** that can be put towards reducing college costs! What an incredible difference a student can make by working only 20 hours a week.

The lesson we get from these studies is that students can do well academically and have a positive impact on their lives by working 10 to 20 hours a week. (Not so surprising, *Upromise Inc.* also found that having a student work 35 hours or more per week is "counterproductive.")

There are two exceptions we would make when it comes to having a student work. First, if a student is already struggling balancing out their studying and/or athletics. Second, if they are receiving a lot of need-based financial aid in the form of gift aid (free money, not loans). Every dollar above $6400* your child earns, counts at 50% against the financial aid they will receive. If your child receives a lot of need-based aid, we would only recommend he/she earn up to $6400. Two excellent books to consider that talk more about this college funding

Apply for financial aid, even if you think you will not qualify. And remember, some colleges require students to complete these forms if they want to be considered for merit aid. – Coach Ryan

strategy are *Debt-Free U* by Zac Bissonnette or *College Aid for Middle-Class America: Solutions to Paying Wholesale vs. Retail* by Ryan Clark.

Option #7 – Using a Combination of Options 1-6

Please realize that one size DOES NOT fit all students and parents. Often families have to use a combination of strategies to cover their college funding needs. By integrating and coordinating multiple strategies, success can be achieved!

More College Funding Ideas:

Every year, families go through the process of filling out financial aid forms in hopes of getting enough money to make college affordable for their student(s). The type of financial aid a student receives totally depends on the students and parents income and assets and of the type of college a student applies to. In some cases, you may discover that most of the financial aid a student receives is in the form of loans.

REMEMBER: Everything begins with the Expected Family Contribution (EFC) of the family.

Assuming you already read through Chapter 16, you know that the EFC is computed by using family financial data submitted on the FAFSA financial aid application form. Private colleges may choose to also use the CSS Profile and/or their own Institutional Methodology (IM). The EFC is then subtracted from the Total Cost of Attendance (tuition, fees, room and board, books and supplies, personal expenses, and transportation to and from college) to arrive at the student's "need", or eligibility for financial aid.

Let's look at an Example:

Johnny wants to attend XYZ Private College. Johnny's EFC is $20,000. The cost of college is $40,000 per year. XYZ College offers Johnny $10,000 in grant money and $5,500 in student loans.

Question – Is this an attractive financial aid offer?

Answer – Maybe. It depends on the college and the student.

Question – Does this offer make college affordable for the family?

Answer – The answer all depends on how this family has planned to pay for college through the years. If they have little to no savings, then this offer **does not** meet the family's financial need of $24,500 ($40k - $10K Grant - $5,500 Student Loan).

You see, the real problem is Johnny's family must still come up with the $24,500 per year to pay the balance due to the college. He was accepted academically to this private college BUT rejected financially!

What can this family do?

Johnny's parents could apply for a parent (PLUS) loan and assuming they qualify for this loan could cover the balance owed to the college. (Currently at a fixed interest rate of 6.84%.) If his parents cannot qualify for the loan, then Johnny will get access to up to an additional $4,000 of Student Loans. This will leave a $20,500 remaining shortfall!

18

HOW is Johnny's family going to cover the rest, the shortfall?

Tough decisions will have to be made if this private college is going to be a **financial fit** for Johnny and his family. Here are a couple of examples of some tough solutions.

- Mom and Dad could take out a loan or a distribution from their retirement accounts but this puts their future in jeopardy. Many families ask about this strategy every year but **WE DO NOT RECOMMEND THIS FUNDING STRATEGY!**
- Johnny could decide to forego his dream of going to the private college and instead attend a different public college or university that he also applied and got accepted to. However, with an average cost of $20,000 and a family EFC of $20,000, Johnny still might have a deficit to cover, less the $5,500 Student Loan he can take out.

Here are some financial strategies families can consider IF they plan EARLY!

- **Cash Flow Strategies** – Use Chapter 17 to map out how your family can pay for as much college as possible from cash flow.
- **Tax Strategies** – Talk to your CPA to see if there are future tax credits you will receive or maximize the tax advantages (savings) of a Small Business.
- **Investment Strategies** – You may be able to uncover hidden costs that can be saved and redirected toward college.
- **EFC Strategies** – When appropriate, it may be possible to reduce your EFC to help increase Financial Aid eligibility at colleges.
- **Loan Strategies** – Reduce your education debt so that parents do not jeopardize their current budget, credit ratings, or retirement savings.

Important Questions to Answer at this Point

In this chapter we have talked about the many ways that students and parents pay for college. If you have done your homework in Chapter 16 (Calculating your EFC) and Chapter 17 (Building your College Budget) you will hopefully be prepared to answer the following questions:

- Have you taken the time to think through and plan how your family is going to pay for college? (Chapter 16 and 17)
- What is your backup plan IF your student does not qualify for enough or any free money (scholarships or grants)? (Chapter 21)
- Will your only alternative be taking out loans (student and parent) and potentially going into considerable debt?
- Will mom and dad have to tap into their savings and retirement funds to help cover college expenses?

Let's face it, the vast majority of families have not been able to save much if any money to help offset the ever increasing cost of college. It is in these cases that important choices need to be made. We didn't say paying for college was going to be easy or come without some sacrifices by parents and students. However, even in this day of high college costs, a student can indeed graduate from college *debt free*. Are you willing to do whatever it takes to make this happen?

By taking action today, you can design a college funding game plan to cover the True Cost of college. Remember, this is a commitment for a minimum of 4 years so plan wisely. **It is all about picking the right college at the right price and having the right funding plan in place.**

> *Every family needs to take the time to talk about the elephant sitting in the room. HOW are you going to pay for college? The earlier you have this conversation the better so that realistic colleges are visited and applied to in the future. DO NOT WAIT!*
> *– Coach Dan*

Continue on to Chapter 19 where you will learn how to find more money to help pay for college!

Please visit Coach Dan's website www.collegeandbeyondllc and Coach Ryan's website www.collegeaidformiddleclass.com if you need help with your college funding game plan!

College Scholarship Search and Log

"The only place success comes before work, is in the dictionary."

- Vince Lombardi, Player & Coach

There are 2 types of College Scholarships:

- Need-Based
- Merit-Based

Need-Based Scholarships and Grants are given to students based on the results of their **Expected Family Contribution (EFC)**. The lower a family's EFC, the more likely a student might receive need-based financial aid from a college. You must do your homework using an EFC Calculator, and a college's Net Price Calculator, and by reviewing a college's historical financial aid details (on www.collegeboard.org) to understand what percentage of money given out by your future college(s) will be in the form of scholarships and grants (FREE money), loans (DEBT money), or work-study. **More details about this are in Chapter 16.**

QuestBridge brings some of the nation's brightest, under-served youth together with leading institutions of higher education. According to their website:

"QuestBridge provides a single, internet-based meeting point which links exceptional students with colleges, scholarship providers, enrichment programs, employers, and organizations seeking students who have excelled despite obstacles. By facilitating these exchanges, QuestBridge aims to increase the percentage of talented low-income students attending the nation's best universities and the ranks of national leadership itself."

Merit-Based College Scholarships represent approximately 75% of the total scholarship dollars awarded every year. Students receive scholarships for:

- Athletics
- Academics
- Talent

NOTE: The most selective colleges **DO NOT** give out any merit-based scholarships (WHY because they have plenty of applicants), however they do offer need based scholarships and grants.

Do you have what the colleges are looking for when it comes to qualifying for top scholarships?

In some cases, scholarships are GUARANTEED based on a student achieving a specific GPA and Test Score to qualify for the scholarship money the college gives out.

In many cases however, having high academics just makes a student ELIGIBLE for some range of scholarship dollars from a college (minimum to a full-ride).

IF you are hoping to receive a top Academic Scholarship, remember that the competition is fierce as more and more students are graduating with high GPA's, high standardized test scores, lots of AP credits, and a bunch of extracurricular activities.

So what are you going to do to make yourself stand out from the rest of the crowd? Having high grades and test scores is NOT ENOUGH.

What is your HOOK?

Students often belong to multiple high school clubs (e.g., Beta Club,Tri-M, DECA, FBLA, FCA, FCCLA) or honor societies (e.g., NHS, Spanish Honor Society, Math Honor Society) which look great on a high school resume. Many of these organizations have a requirement that members have to do so many hours of community service. But a HOOK is something unique that a student does. And a hook is a something ANY student can do IF s/he is willing to do something above and beyond what everybody else is doing. The idea is to focus on making a difference in your community or the world. A HOOK happens when you create, establish or found something of significance like a:

- Foundation
- Small business
- Unique Mission Trip
- One of a kind Community project

The key is that whatever you decide to do MUST be something of which you are passionate and has the potential for legacy, having the ability to be continued in college or handed off to someone else. We also believe that doing something just for the sake of building up your resume will ultimately blowup on you when you can't explain or defend WHY you did it, for example in an interview or essay, so choose wisely!

Local newspapers love to showcase students who have stepped up and taken the initiative to create something of significance and make a difference in their community. Students, reach out to them, share what you are doing OR have someone do it for you. Describe what your student has done, and there is a good chance someone from the newspaper will decide to write an article about your students' project. Everybody loves to read about a student making a difference and the article in the paper will be yet another way to impress those future scholarship judges too.

Private Scholarships represent approximately 25% of the total scholarship dollars awarded every year. Pursuing and researching private scholarships can feel like a full-time job. You should start your scholarship search by reviewing all **local** and **regional** scholarships, then search nationwide for additional scholarships. For example, your chances of winning a local Lion's Club scholarship is usually much higher since there is less competition, than competing nationally for very large scholarships (like those offered by Coca-Cola).

19

Remember, the more zero's behind the dollar amount, the more competition you will face.

Private scholarships are given out for a variety of reasons:

- Leadership skills
- Volunteer hours
- Essay writing ability
- Special interests (hobbies, club membership etc.)
- Random Drawings

When it comes to getting Volunteer or Community Service hours, there are many things you can do. Here are some examples of places where you can volunteer:

- Nursing Homes
- Tutoring a student
- Being a Summer Camp Counselor
- Coaching a youth sports team
- Organizing a Vacation Bible School at your church
- Helping with Church or community dinners, festivals, or parades
- Involvement in Scouting (Girl Scouts, Boy Scouts)

Private College Scholarships are awarded to students by:

- Foundations
- Corporations
- Churches
- Individuals
- Community Groups
- For-Profit and Non-Profit
- Clubs
- Labor Unions

Start your research for private scholarships with your High School Guidance Counselor. Counselors generally receive outside scholarship applications and notifications sometime in the late fall or just after the first of the New Year. In some cases, counselors are asked to nominate students for specific scholarships. Counselors are also tasked with the preliminary assessment of submitted scholarship applications. Make your interest and presence known so that when they are making their final selections, they think of you first!

Finally, narrow your search for scholarships that match what you do outside of high school. To help you with this process, complete the **Scholarship Inventory (see below)**. Your answers will help you concentrate on specific opportunities.

Moreover, your answers can also help to identify your **weakest areas**: grades test scores, community service, etc. To fill any gaps, it is important for you to find something that you are passionate about and TAKE ACTION! Do something that makes you UNIQUE and helps to set you apart from the rest of the applicants. Pursue scholarships that match your: leadership skills, community service, attributes, academic success, talents or other terrific skills.

Side Note: When it comes time to search for private scholarships, focus your time on targeting specific scholarship opportunities. Remember, every free scholarship dollar received is one less dollar that comes out of your pocket OR that you and your family potentially have to take out in college loans. For example, one of our students was a member of a Scholastic Trap Shooting Team, and so he researched, applied for, and received two scholarships totaling $7,500. It was his sport that made him eligible to apply for and receive these particular scholarships. He also knew that the odds were in his favor because there were a limited number of applicants. To this student's credit, he had everything they were looking for: registered member of a competitive trap shooting team, high academics, and he followed the rules specified on the application.

In another case, a student decided to focus on going after scholarships given to high school students who plan to become a teacher. She applied for ten scholarships and received three scholarships totaling $10,000!

Both of these students identified areas in their lives that made them unique and targeted specific scholarships they were qualified to win. What a great return on their invested time!

Remember, one of the worst things you can do is procrastinate when it comes to searching and applying for college scholarships, so start your strategic scholarship search today!

Complete this <u>Scholarship Inventory</u> and TAKE ACTION!

1. Do you have a hobby or talent that makes you stand out?

   -
   -
   -
   -

2. What subjects do you enjoy or excel in at high school? What about your writing skills?

   -
   -
   -
   -

19

3. Do you know what your future career path (major) will be in college?

   -
   -
   -
   -

4. Have you started a business, foundation, or personally organized a community project?

   -
   -
   -
   -

5. Have you calculated your Expected Family Contribution (EFC) number? If so, will you receive need-based financial aid (grants or scholarships)?

   -
   -
   -
   -

6. Are you an academic superstar (high GPA and Test Scores) at your high school, have a desire to go to an Ivy League College but have no money for college (low EFC and on Free and Reduced Lunch)? If so, should you consider applying to QuestBridge?

   -
   -
   -
   -

7. Do your parents employers or organizations they belong to give out College Scholarships?

   -
   -
   -
   -

8. Does your employer offer College Scholarships?

   -
   -
   -
   -

9. Does your ethnicity or family heritage make you eligible for college scholarships?

   -
   -
   -
   -

10. What makes you unique?

   -
   -
   -
   -

College Scholarship Log

Which Scholarships are you hoping to receive? Track your Results BELOW:

Scholarship Name	Amount	Requirements	Due Date
Total			

19

College Scholarship Websites

www.Google.com (search using Key Words)

www.MyScholly.com (small fee for this one)

www.fastweb.com

www.scholarshippoints.com

www.tuitionfundingsources.com

www.collegescholarships.org

www.studentscholarshipsearch.com

www.findtuition.com

www.unigo.com

www.CollegeAnswer.com/scholarships

www.collegedata.com

www.finaid.org

www.cappex.com

www.chegg.com/scholarships

www.petersons.com

www.salliemae.com

www.careeronestop.org/findtraining/pay/scholarships

www.scholarships.com

http://collegeapps.about.com/od/grantsandscholarships/

www.schoolsoup.com

Remember to visit Coach Dan's website www.collegeandbeyondllc.com
and Coach Ryan's website www.collegeaidformiddleclass.com
to find additional resources on this important topic!

After you have completed all your application, take a look again at your local community scholarships. It is a great time to revisit those opportunities. — *Coach Ryan*

Looking for scholarships can become a full time job. Parents often become an active participant when a student is over committed. Pursue scholarships matching a student's resume of activities and accomplishments and realize the big money is at the colleges themselves. — *Coach Dan*

19

College Visits and Evaluations

"Be more concerned with your character than your reputation, because your character is what you really are, while your reputation is merely what others think you are."

- John Wooden, Coach

One of the primary goals of a college visit is to make sure the college is a good "social" fit for the student. In other words, a student does not want the "personality" of the college to be so dramatically different than their own personality. Making these visits will give you a clearer picture of the setup and size of the school and a better view of the social environment.

This is invaluable information because this will help your student determine if the campus is "good enough" for them and is it a place where they can thrive, (not just survive) during their college years. Please remember, there is no such thing as a perfect college. Every college has its pluses and minuses. You are not looking for the perfect college. Your job during the college visit is to identify if each school is a place where your student can succeed and blossom during these critical years.

Ideally we recommend you visit on a weekday at a time when school is in session. This will give you a better opportunity to see the dynamics and feel of what a typical day will be like at each college and get an idea of the diversity of the student body on campus.

It is also important that you track and evaluate each school based on a two part ranking system.

Part I

The first part is a way for you to rank each college based on relevant factors for each of the colleges you choose to visit. This ranking is an excellent way to help you narrow down your final college selection and give you the ability to have an objective scoring system that tracks how you feel about each of the colleges you visit.

Part II

The second part of the evaluation is a list of strategic questions you should consider asking during your college visits. You should be interviewing the Admissions Officer, Financial Aid Officer, faculty involved in the student's major, other students on campus, Career Placement Officer, and any coaches if you are planning on playing a sport. While the admissions office will determine if a student is admitted into their school, you also need to decide if the college or university is acceptable to you. You want to find out as much as you can about the school while

20

you are on campus. This will help you identify the true nature of each school and identify which college is right for you. **Remember** this college needs to fit you: academically, financially, socially, and geographically.

- *Make copies of the following pages for each of your college visits.*
- *Take them with you and take notes during and after so that you can remember important details.*
- *It is best to ask the questions in your own words versus reading them directly off the page.*

20

Part I: As you visit colleges, it is important to track what you like and dislike about each of them.

(Rate everything on a Scale of 0 to 10 with 0 being "TERRIBLE" and 10 being "EXCELLENT". Use N/A if not pertinent)

	College Name	College Name	College Name	College Name	College Name	College Name	College Name	College Name	College Name	College Name
Location										
Size										
Campus Setting										
Weather										
Students										
Faculty										
Food										
Dorm Room										
Facilities										
Sports										
Talent Programs										
Special Programs										
Co-op Programs										
Religion										
Student/Faculty Ratio										
Diversity										
Greek System										
Campus Safety										
Other / Misc.										
Overall Experience										
Total										

PART II: Questions to be addressed: Please score on how satisfied you are with the answer you received from the school official(s):
(Great Answer-3pts, Good Answer-2pts, Poor/Not Responsive-1pt)
At the end of each questionnaire, add up your scores and place it in the box marked "Total Score

ADMISSIONS QUESTIONNAIRE

College Name: _____ Date: _____

Questions:	Answers:	Score (1,2,3)
What are the most important criteria used for admissions?		
How are these criteria ranked by admissions?		
How important is the SAT/ACT test?		
What are the different admission deadlines?		
What is the four year graduation rate?		
What is the six year graduation rate?		
What percentage of freshman will graduate?		
Does the college major play a role in the graduation rate?		
How hard is it to sign up for classes?		
What percentage of graduates will go on to graduate school?		
Other Questions:		
	Total Score:	

FINANCIAL AID QUESTIONNAIRE

(Great Answer-3pts, Good Answer-2pts, Poor/Not Responsive-1pt)

College Name: _____   **Date:** _____

Questions:	Answers:	Score(1,2,3)
What financial aid forms are required?		
Are you a need blind school?		
What is the college's financial aid deadline?		
Do you have a different deadline for Early Action or Early Decision?		
Do you use financial aid leveraging?		
What % of financial need do you meet?		
Is needs assessment tied to merit awards?		
What is the total cost of college per year at your school?		
What non-direct billed items are included in this number?		
What other non-need based aid is available?		
If I am awarded a private scholarship, will the school add or subtract the scholarship		
What is the average amount of debt incurred by each student upon graduation?		
What is the average amount of debt incurred by the parents upon graduation?		
Other Questions:		

20

CAREER PLACEMENT QUESTIONNAIRE

(Great Answer-3pts, Good Answer-2pts, Poor/Not responsive-1pt

College Name: _____ **Date:** _____

Questions:	Answers:	Score(1,2,3)
What job placement services does the college provide?		
How many work full-time?		
Can graduates use the services after graduation?		
What college majors are being recruited the heaviest and easiest to employ?		
What majors are having difficulty finding jobs?		
What percentage of students find jobs before graduation?		
Are there any companies that recruit graduates? Which ones?		
Does the faculty assist in helping students get job?		
Are careers fairs held during the year?		
Are there any credentials that seem to help students a find job quicker?		
What is the future employment outlook for my major?		
What is the starting salary for my major?		
Other Questions:		
	Total Score:	

FACULTY QUESTIONNAIRE

(Great Answer-3pts, Good Answer-2pts, Poor/Not Responsive-1pt)

College Name: _____   **Date:** _____

Questions:	Answers:	Score(1,2,3)
How many years should it take to graduate in this program?		
Does this department have any special programs, facilities, or technology?		
Does the faculty assist in helping students find internships or co-ops?		
Are faculty available after class to answer questions?		
Do full time professors teach introductory classes? What percentage?		
What percentage of full time professors are on staff?		
Would it be possible to sit in on a class?		
What is the average size of the classes?		
What advice would you give to a high school student?		
Overall impression of the faculty and department at this school		
Other Questions:		
	Total Score:	

20

COLLEGE STUDENT QUESTIONNAIRE

(Great Answer-3pts, Good Answer-2pts, Poor/Not Responsive-1pt)

College Name: _____ **Date:** _____

Questions:	Answers:	Score (1,2,3)
What is your overall feeling about the school?		
What do you like most?		
What do you like least?		
On a scale of 1-10, 1 being very liberal & 10 very conservative, how would you rate the faculty?		
What are the classes like?		
Are professors easy to speak with?		
How many students are in your class on average?		
Impressions of campus life and social life?		
Do most students go home on the weekends or stay on campus?		
How do you like your dorm?		
Any general advice you can give me on preparing for my freshman year?		
Other Questions:		
	Total Score:	

COACH/ATHLETIC DEPARTMENT QUESTIONNAIRE

(Great Answer-3pts, Good Answer-2pts, Poor/Not Responsive-1pt)

College Name: _____ Date: _____

Questions:	Answers:	Score(1,2,3)
How supportive are your fans?		
Do you share any facilities with any other sport?		
Are any new facilities planned to be completed over the coming years?		
What does a typical day look like for an athlete?		
Can you review the off-season workout schedule?		
Where will the team be traveling to next year?		
Does everyone make the traveling team?		
How many coaches are on staff?		
How many trainers are on staff?		
What is the opportunity for me to play at my position?		
Do you have specific team rules or policies?		
What class and exam allowances are in place for athletes?		
Are tutors available if assistance is needed in a subject?		
Will I be able to travel home for the holidays?		
Overall Impressions:		
Other Questions		
	Total Score:	

20

Cumulative SCORING CHART After Each College Visit

Now it is time to add up all of your Total Scores: Transfer over the Total Scores from each sheet to this CUMMULATIVE SCORING CHART.

College Name	Total Part	Total Part I Ranking	Total Admission Questionnaire	Total Financial Aid Questionnaire	Total Career Placement Questionnaire	Total Faculty Questionnaire	Total Student Questionnaire	Total Coach Questionnaire	Total Score
College Name									
1									
2									
3									
4									
5									
6									
7									
8									
9									
10									
11									
12									
13									
14									
15									
16									

Ranking the Colleges

Now it is time to **RANK your colleges from HIGHEST to LOWEST.** This will help you determine which colleges best fit your student's personality and the family's expectations. If you are unable to visit a college, make sure you look for some online "Virtual" college visits. If you do not like the virtual college tours, you will not like the campus, so don't waste your time visiting a college if you were not impressed with the virtual tour. Make it a point to attend a few College Fairs in your area so you can speak with the admissions representatives at the colleges you are considering visiting and applying to in the future. Alumni can also be an excellent resource for you to learn about the colleges you are considering as well.

Stretch (Reach) colleges are places you may have a tough time getting admitted into academically or financially. **Safety** or **Fallback** colleges are schools to which you will definitely get admitted and can afford. Students also sometimes have **50/50** colleges where it could go either way

20

Ranking	College Name	Stretch, Safe, Fall Back?
1		
2		
3		
4		
5		
6		
7		
8		
9		
10		
11		
12		
13		
14		
15		

Summer college visits are not ideal, but necessary. If it is a school you really like, make sure you visit the college again when students return to get a better feel for the campus and academic life. – *Coach Ryan*

The best way to decide if a college is a good fit for a student socially (and we're not talking toga party) is to visit the campus. Some colleges allow a student to spend the night so do your research and plan accordingly. – *Coach Dan*

Remember to visit Coach Dan's website www.collegeandbeyondllc.com and Coach Ryan's website www.collegeaidformiddleclass.com

College Selection & Final College List

"You're the only one who can make the difference. Whatever your dream is, go for it!"
- Magic Johnson, NBA Player & Coach

Some Colleges Offer an Outstanding Education...and Money!

With over 3,000 four-year colleges to choose from, it might seem that selecting an elite (and expensive) college or university would help to leverage your personal and professional success. If this were the case, then choosing an Ivy League or Top-25 school would virtually guarantee those students an edge over other graduates in the workforce.

However, there is no evidence that any school provides the right mix of factors to ensure personal and professional success. The only statistic available that shows the value of a college degree comes from a census study that was done by the federal government back in the year 2012, which indicates that the average college graduate can expect to earn about $1,000,000 more than a high school graduate over their working lifetime.

In reality, though, an Ivy League degree does not guarantee anything except the short-term branding of one's perceived quality or value as a person or an employee. There is no research that suggests an Ivy League college degree provides more earning potential over a lifetime, more happiness, more insight, more knowledge, or more self-worth-per-dollar-spent than any other school in the country. Actually, a study by Forbes magazine revealed that among the CEOs of leading Fortune 300 corporations, 87% did not attend a Top 25 school for their under-graduate studies.

The fact remains that most college students do not attend elite colleges, regardless of the "nameplate" or "brand" of the school they choose to attend. Many colleges offer tremendous value, depending upon the needs, wants, and values that an individual student is looking for in his or her college search. Furthermore, you'll find many corporate, foundation, and civic leaders who graduated from less selective public and private schools too.

And What about the Money?

Many colleges offer significant grants, scholarships, and tuition discounts to attract quality students, regardless of the family's income or financial need. Ivy League schools, on the other hand, only offer financial aid to families who have a financial need.

Students enter college from various socioeconomic backgrounds. Then they graduate into a workforce with a specific set of skills, knowledge, and attitude shaped by very diverse experiences. No two graduates are alike, and no two schools are alike. Just remember, the right college choice can make a big difference in a student's future; however, the wrong college choice could cost a bundle and leave a student with emotional and financial regrets for years.

Parents, if you have a junior or senior who is struggling with picking the right college for their future, AND the family budget; please contact our offices today. We can help them navigate their way through the process, which can have a BIG impact on your pocketbook!

Time to create your <u>Final College Short List</u> of where you will be applying:

1. _____

2. _____

3. _____

4. _____

5. _____

6. _____

7. _____

8. _____

9. _____

10. _____

Continue on to Chapter 22 and take action today!

To schedule a meeting, visit Coach Dan's website www.collegeandbeyondllc.com and Coach Ryan's website www.collegeaidformiddleclass.com

Select your recommenders carefully. The best teachers to ask are those who liked you in class and where you worked really hard.
— *Coach Ryan*

All of your hard work comes down to picking your final college. Take the time to look at the pros and cons of each school and then go with the facts and your gut. Which one fits you the best financially, academically, socially, and geographically? Best of luck!
— *Coach Dan*

21

College Resume &
Letters of Recommendation

"Be more concerned with your character than your reputation. Because your character is what you really are, while your reputation is merely what others think you are."

– John Wooden, Basketball Coach

It is important that you create a *College Resume* for a number of reasons.

- **First**, it allows you to list all of your Academic Successes, Awards, Honors, Leadership Positions, Sports, Community Service (volunteer), Activities (clubs, organizations) and Work Experience. This is an opportunity to see where your strengths lie and where you can further develop your talents and leadership abilities.
- **Second**, a Resume is a great item to give to teachers, counselors and/or other adults who know you well and have made an impact on your life (also called centers-of-influence) and whom you plan to ask to write letters of recommendation. This will help them know more about your outside accomplishments, interests, and activities.
- **Third**, some colleges allow you to attach a Resume to provide additional insight during the application process.
- **Finally**, creating and updating your Resume is a great habit to get into during high school because eventually you are going to need a solid Resume for future internship, co-op, and job opportunities.

22

On the following pages, we have provided you with a few sample resumes to consider as you build your own. Pick the format you prefer or consider using a preformatted computer resume program you can find by doing an online search or in use by your guidance counselor.

Ideally your Resume should not exceed one page or a page and a half UNLESS you have extensive accomplishments that need to be shared (e.g., multiple volunteer activities, talent [drama, music], athletics, academics, awards, jobs).

Remember to visit Coach Dan's website www.collegeandbeyondllc.com
and Coach Ryan's website www.collegeaidformiddleclass.com

Resume Template with Descriptions of Each Section

First and Last Name

123 Main Street
Anytown, NC 12345
E-mail: noemail@gmail.com
Home Phone: (123) 456-7890

Educational/Career Goals: Concisely state what your educational goals are for college. You should state what you plan to study and what you hope to do with the degree you obtain (e.g., My educational goal is to obtain a bachelor's degree in Early Childhood Education and a minor in English. I hope to use this degree to teach, do research, and work with underprivileged children.

Academic History:

High School: School name, city, year of graduation

Class Rank:

GPA:

Curriculum: List any IB, AP, and honors courses and current and past courses taken.

Senior Year: AP English, AP US History, Spanish IV, Psychology

Junior Year: AP English, World Civilization, Spanish III, AP Chemistry

Sophomore Year: Honors English, American Government, Spanish II, AP Biology

Freshman Year: AP Human Geography, Honors English, World History

Achievements or Honors: Make sure you describe the award in detail but make it concise. You should tell the name of the award, how it was given out, and the criteria that you met to achieve the award. Be specific and use bullet points.

Extracurricular Activities: Make subcategories for all of your school related activities. Use bullet points for each activity in the sub-category. Describe any leadership positions you held, what you added by being involved with this group, or how you benefited from being involved.

Sports: Take the time to describe your involvement in sports and the number of years you have been dedicated to the sport. Also include any awards you have received, without duplicating what you already mentioned above.

Community Service: Make subcategories for any volunteer opportunities and community service you performed. Also include activities like Boy Scouts/Girl Scouts and other community groups. Explain leadership roles, duties, responsibilities, and your participation in the groups. List the number of hours or the amount of time committed to each activity and the years you participated.

Personal Interest: Have you dedicated any time or energy following your passions? Make a statement about a subject matter of which you are passionate. How have these passions helped you grow, develop, and enhance your personality and future college major and career aspirations?

Employment: Bullet point any jobs you have held, dates, and responsibilities.

Travel: Do you have any unusual travel and foreign language skills? (e.g., Have traveled with my family to a number of European Countries including _____, Am fluent in speaking French.)

22

SAMPLE RESUME #1

John Doe
123 Main Street
Anytown, NC 12345
E-mail: noemail@gmail.com
Home Phone: (123) 456-7890

Educational/Career Goals:

My educational goal is to obtain a Bachelor's Degree in Communications from the University of USA. My career goal is to become a writer.

Academic History:

School: Anytown High School, Anytown, North Carolina—Graduate 20XX

Class Rank: 11th of 389 students

GPA: 3.95

Curriculum: College Preparation
Advanced Placement-English Language
Honors English I, II, III, IV
Honors Civics/ Economics
Honors World History
Honors U.S. History
Honors Biology
Honors Chemistry
Pre-Calculus
Spanish I, II, III

Achievements or Honors:

Lions Club Top 10 Honoree: Award given by the Lion's club for students who have a minimum GPA of 3.0 and participate in a high school sport, and show strong leadership in their community. Only one student is awarded this per year in my high school.

Personal Interests:

Basketball/ Football/Travel

Extracurricular Activities:

        Editor-in-Chief—Anytown High School Newspaper
        Drama Club
        Student Council
        Basketball—4 years (Captain)
        Football—4 years (Captain)

Community Service:

        Prayer Partner - Epworth United Methodist Church (UMC), Uptown, NC
        Fall Festival Children's Volunteer - UMC, Uptown, NC
        Operation Christmas Child Shoe Box Volunteer- UMC, Uptown, NC

Employment:

        Food Lion, Anytown, NC - March 20XX until present _____

References:

        Reverend John Doe, United Methodist Church, johndoe@gmail.com, cell: 555-122-1234, 100 Burrage Road NE, Anytown NC, 12894

        Laure Smith, English Teacher & Varsity Girls' Basketball Coach, High School, laure.smith@anytownhighschool.edu, cell# 123-456-7899, 987 School Road, Anytown, NC 12435

22

SAMPLE RESUME #2

Sandy A. Sunshine

sandysunshine@yahoo.com
1234 Happy Rd.
Happyville, KY 41094
134-222-2222

Mainville High School
Weighted GPA: 4.05
Unweighted GPA: 3.86
Graduating: May 2016

EXTRACURRICULAR ACTIVITIES

- **Band**
  - Played clarinet as a hobby
- **Cheerleading**
  - Been a cheerleader for 8 years
  - Volunteered at Elementary School to teach children new cheers and routines
- **National Honor Society**
  - A member from junior year to present
  - Must complete 20 hours of community service each semester
- **Math Honor Society**
  - A member from junior year to present
  - Must complete 10 hours of community service each year; two hours must be math tutoring
- **English Honor Society**
  - A member for my senior year
  - Must complete 10 hours of community service each year
- **FBLA – Future Business Leaders of America**
  - A member from freshman year to present

SPORTS

- **Track and Field**
  - Competed on JV team sophomore year and ran in open 100 and 200 meter race
  - Placed sixth at the last meet of the season in the open 100 meter run
- **Gymnastics**
  - Tumbled for 13 years in floor and trampoline for Top Gymnastics Team
  - Volunteered once a month to help teach pre-school children basic tasks of tumbling

LEADERSHIP POSITIONS

- ➢ Chairperson of Fundraising
  - ○ Junior year became the Chairperson of Fundraising of FBLA
  - ○ Had to organize our annual spaghetti dinner as our fundraiser.
    - ▪ Raised $5,000.00
- ➢ Vice President
  - ○ Senior year became Vice President of FBLA
  - ○ In charge of the spaghetti dinner again this year
  - ○ Taught leadership class at the University of Kentucky for the FBLA retreat

WORK EXPERIENCE

Fuel and Food Pantry
Assistant Manager *August 2010 – July 2012*

- ➢ Worked as a waitress in the restaurant
- ➢ Worked as a cashier and fuel desk attendant

Cinema Duplex
Cashier at Concession Stand *May 2013-Present*

- ➢ *Processing food orders for customers*
- ➢ *Helped cooking staff on occasion*

HONORS AND AWARDS

- ➢ Received a positive referral freshman year for voluntarily tutoring my peers in math
- ➢ Chosen each year to attend meetings hosted by the People to People Organization

COMMUNITY SERVICE

- ➢ Worked at a local Food Pantry to help disadvantaged families
- ➢ Volunteered at St. Johns Hospital in the Emergency Room, helping to stock supplies
- ➢ Worked at our church festival where I managed the kids' games

22

SAMPLE RESUME #3

Sample Student
234 Mary Way
Sample, City 12345
anygirl@gmail.com
(123) 456-7891

Magic High School
Graduating: June 2017
Weighted GPA: 3.658
Unweighted GPA: 3.538

HONORS, AWARDS, AND MEMBERSHIPS

- **Cheerleading MVP Award** - 9th grade
- **CHL All Star Award** - 9th and 10th grade
- **Latin Honor Society** – 11th and 12th grade
- **National Society of High School Scholars** – 11th and 12th grade
- **Scholar Athlete Award-** 9th, 10th 11th grade
- **Cum Laude Award-** Awarded during my junior year for the National Latin Exam
- **National Honor Society** – 11th and 12th grade
- **UCA All American Cheerleader** – 9th grade
- **Cheerleading-** member of the JV squad in the fall of 2011, a member of the Varsity squad in the winter of 2011 up to present day, and Captain of the Cheerleading team 11th & 12th
- **Trained Student Leader TSL-** A program designed to help incoming freshmen with the transition from middle school to high school. I was selected to be part of the program from the start of my junior year through present day.
- **Key Club-** 9th ,11th ,12th
- **Spanish Club-** 9th
- **Latin Club-** 10th , 11th
- **Revive Club-** 12th ; service based youth

COMMUNITY SERVICE

- **Freshman Year -** 17 hours
  - St. Jude Children's Hospital Walk
  - Freestore Foodbank
  - Hartzell Church Fish fry
- **Sophomore Year -** 21 hours
  - Happy Church's Vacation Bible School
  - Classroom assistance and set up at Liberty Heights Elementary School
  - Kindervelt fundraiser
- **Junior Year -** 92 hours
  - Stepping Stones Summer Camp
  - Delivering Meals at Meals on Wheels
  - Classroom assistance and set up at Gold Elementary
  - Happy Church Fish fry
- **Senior Year -** 46.5 hours (In Progress)
  - Classroom assistance and set up at Liberty Elementary School

Letter of Recommendation TIPS

When it comes to getting letters of recommendation, please keep the following items in mind:

- **WHO** you ask to write a letter for you is **IMPORTANT**. Remember, you want to pick someone whom you feel really knows you, is a good writer (YES, grammar and punctuation count for these individuals too!), and will give you the accolades you deserve. **CAUTION**: you must have confidence in this person's ability to build you up on paper, not tear you down without you knowing it, so pick wisely!

- **WHAT** is the letter of recommendation for? Is it for a college application, honors program or a scholarship? This can make a big difference in the way your recommender writes their letter. Make sure your recommender knows who the audience is going to be so that they can write something that is appropriate.

- **WHEN** do you need to approach your teachers, counselors, and other recommenders for their letters of recommendation? **ASAP!** If the people you identify are popular recommenders then you need to be at the top of their pile, not the bottom. We encourage you to approach these individuals in the spring of your junior year. Waiting until the first week of your senior year may be too late especially if you are applying to competitive colleges. Check in with your high school counselor.

- **WHERE** should they send their letters of recommendation? Again check with your high school counselor to see if there is a specific protocol when it comes to processing letters of recommendation. High Schools using Naviance or Parchment often require that these letters be sent directly (electronically) to the counselor's office so they can be electronically sent out with other application requirements (Official Transcripts, School Profile Letters, Counselor Letters of Recommendation etc.). In addition, IF you are using the Common Application or the Coalition Application to apply to your colleges, ALL letters of recommendation MUST be submitted electronically.

- **HOW** can you help your recommenders know more about you? We suggest you give each of them a copy of your RESUME where you have listed everything in which you have been involved over the years, outside the classroom. This will help them personalize your letter. When it comes to making sure letters are processed in a timely fashion, the key is to be pleasantly persistent in checking in with those whom you asked to write your letters. Teachers and other recommenders are busy and sometimes forget that there is a DEADLINE for when these letters need to be completed and submitted. It is OK to check in with them from time to time, just don't get pushy OR they may reflect this in the letter they write for you. Make it a point, once you receive their letter of

22

recommendation, to send this individual a hand-written thank you note, card, or letter and also send one to other school staff members who has helped you in college process!

- **WHY** do you need letters of recommendation and do you always need them? Letters of Recommendation are often used by Admissions Counselors and Scholarship Committees as a way to differentiate an applicant from the rest of the crowd. In this day and age of fierce competition, when it comes to getting admitted to the most prestigious colleges or receiving the most competitive scholarships, letters of recommendation (and essays) may be the magic that puts a student over the top with the selection committee. However, remember that not all colleges or scholarships require a letter of recommendation. Some even limit the number you can submit. Do your research after you have selected your Short List of Colleges to determine whether or not a letter of recommendation is expected or encouraged. Sometimes OPTIONAL can be a necessity, so just do it!

Student Questionnaire

In addition to the Student Resume, you might want to consider answering the following questions about yourself and giving this information to the individuals who will be writing your letters of recommendation. By completing the questions below, you will ensure your letter writers are fully aware of all your accomplishments.

We have included EXAMPLES to help get you started:

1. **List three words that describe you both individually and scholastically.**
   a. Unique
   b. Eager learner
   c. Self -starter

2. **What subject(s) or course(s) have been or currently are your favorite(s), regardless of how well you did? Please explain why you enjoyed the course(s) and give specific examples of what you found compelling.**

   a. I loved Mrs. Clark's World History class. Once the class began, I found myself not only reading the textbook, but checking out related books from the library to learn more about the various historical events. I loved reading on my own and I received an A in the class.

3. **What would you consider your biggest academic obstacle or difficulty? What specifically have you done or implemented to help you with this weakness?**

   a. During my freshman year of high school, I waited until the last minute to complete all of my written assignments. This caused me to stay up late at night completing assignments, lose valuable sleep, and add additional stress to my already hectic schedule. I learned my lesson and I began my sophomore year with a new objective: complete my written assignments as soon as possible. I now get a lot more sleep and my schedule is much more manageable once I stopped procrastinating.

4. **How would you describe yourself as a student? Please give an example of an accolade and/or accomplishment in high school you are proud of receiving. What makes you feel proud about receiving this award?**

   a. Dedicated is the word I would use to describe myself as a student. I started in the Cub Scouts when I was a first grader. I went on to become a Webelos and a Boy Scout as I got older. My goal since being a young first grade Cub Scout was to achieve the rank of Eagle Scout. I worked very hard this past summer on my Eagle Scout project to help needy families in the country of Jamaica get medical help. I worked with a local eye doctor and collected over a thousand used eye glasses that he could re-use to help individuals in Jamaica receive the gift of sight. I spent the last ten years of my life working toward my goal, and I was able reach the rank of Eagle Scout in June.

22

5. **Explain a time when you have changed your opinion, attitude, or perspective based upon a teacher/class/book/experience etc. How and why did it change you?**

   a. During the first grading period of my freshman year, I was shocked by how low my grades were. Neither I, nor my parents, were very proud when I showed them my grades. I knew I could do better and I never wanted my parents to be disappointed in me again. I changed my study habits immediately and have never received a grade less than a "B" since that first grading period.

6. **Think of three individuals who you would like to ask to write you a letter of recommendation. The first and second recommenders should be teachers from your high school and from an academic subject. Finally, the last individual should be a member of the community who knows you well outside of the classroom.**

One final suggestion: The Common Application will ask you to voluntarily give up your right to read any of your written letters of recommendation. The colleges and universities feel that they will get an unbiased letter if the student is unable to read the letter before it is sent to the colleges. If you do not give up this right, most colleges will not read or accept your letters of recommendation. Our advice is to go ahead and waive your rights on the Common Application.

Nevertheless, when applying for some outside scholarships or college applications (in which you are not using the Common Application/Universal Application/Coalition Application), you may be asked to provide a copy of a letter of recommendation. It is OK to ask your recommender for a copy BUT be sensitive to the fact that they may not want to share what they wrote on your behalf with you. Offer them the opportunity to place their letter in a sealed envelope and then submit it. Follow the directions listed on the scholarship or college application and choose your recommenders wisely. And again, please remember to send a hand written thank you note, card or letter to your recommenders!

May 1st is your deadline to let a college know that your student will be attending their school. Make sure you let them know by May 1st.
– Coach Ryan

Your college resume is a snap shot of your high school career, so update it regularly. Focus on getting letters of recommendation from terrific teachers you are confident know you and want to see you succeed after high school.
– Coach Dan

The College Essay

"Obstacles don't have to stop you. If you run into a wall, don't turn around and give up. Figure out how to climb it, go through it or work around it."

- Michael Jordan, NBA Player

By Susan Knoppow, CEO, Wow Writing Workshop

What is a College Essay?

You've done the hard work – taken the classes, gotten the grades, prepped for standardized tests. Now it's time to think about applications, and that probably means writing college essays.

The term "college essay" refers to any piece of writing that a school requires as part of the admissions process. Application essays come in all shapes and sizes. They tend to be between 150 and 600 words, and include many different types of prompts. Here are the basics, so you'll feel prepared to dive in and draft great essays.

23

Personal Statements

Most students will write a personal statement, either as part of the Common Application or in another stand-alone application. Personal statements ask for reflection, and include questions like these:

- Some students have a background, identity, interest, or talent that is so meaningful they believe their application would be incomplete without it. If this sounds like you, then please share your story.
- The lessons we take from failure can be fundamental to later success. Recount an incident or time when you experienced failure. How did it affect you, and what did you learn from the experience?
- Tell us about a personal quality, talent, accomplishment, contribution, or experience that is important to you. What about this quality or accomplishment makes you proud and how does it relate to the person you are?
- Describe a significant experience from the past two years which required you to interact with someone outside of your own social or cultural group (ethnic, religious, geographic, socioeconomic, etc.). How did this impact you? What did you learn and what surprised you?
- Describe a circumstance, obstacle or conflict in your life and the skills and resources you used to resolve it. Did it change you? If so, how?

Supplements

In addition to a personal statement, many colleges also require supplemental essays. While some schools, such as the University of Chicago, ask students to respond to a creative prompt, supplements generally fall into three categories:

Activity Essays, which ask you to expand on your involvement in a specific extracurricular activity.

Why College X Essays, which ask you to explain why you are interested in this college or program.

Community Essays, which ask you to describe your role in a particular community, such as a youth group, a sports team or your family.

Other Essays

You might also have to write essays as part of scholarship applications, or for admission into Honors Colleges and other special programs. In many cases, you will be able to modify essays you have already written to address these prompts.

> The hardest part of the college essay is just getting it started. Try not to procrastinate. Summer after your junior year in high school is a good time to gather your thoughts.
>
> — *Coach Ryan*

Tips from the Admissions Office

Regardless of whether you are writing a personal statement or another type of essay, each one gives you a chance to share something meaningful about yourself.

At Wow Writing Workshop, we speak all the time to admissions professionals at top universities across the country, and we know what they are looking for. One thing's for sure: They don't want you to write a story about something you think they want to hear. They do want to read a story you want to share with them.

As Michigan State University Director of Admissions Jim Cotter puts it, the essay is value added.

"At a moderately selective school, it can pull a student on the cusp up," said Cotter, a 30+-year veteran. "At a highly selective school, a poor statement can make the difference between being admitted or not."

Here are a few more tips direct from admissions offices to help you write an essay that could improve your chances of getting noticed, and getting in. While these tips are particularly relevant to personal statements, they offer good general guidelines for any type of application essay.

Keep it simple. "I think sometimes students feel that because they haven't found the cure for cancer they have nothing to share," said **Vanderbilt University Assistant Director for Undergraduate Admissions Jan Deike.** "Life is truly lived in the smaller moments, and that can be a powerful essay."

> Colleges often use the college essay as the final decision piece in making the difficult choice between two qualified applicants so take it seriously. Give them a reason to remember your essay, for all the right reasons. — *Coach Dan*

Know your audience. "There's a misconception about what we do inside the admissions office. We are trying to predict future potential," said **Johns Hopkins University Senior Associate Director for Undergraduate Admissions Calvin Wise.** "The essay is a student's opportunity to speak directly to the admissions office. That's where we find out more about the student."

Understand the prompt. "Answer the question," said **Shawn Felton, Cornell University Director of Undergraduate Admissions.** "Since so many students don't do that, you could actually stand out by doing that very basic thing."

Stay focused. "Students do not need to compile an entire season into an essay," according to **Lorenzo Gamboa, Associate Director of Undergraduate Admissions at Santa Clara University.** "Just give us one place, one time, one moment, and that will do it for you. The key is to show genuine passion, commitment, and that you have what it takes to survive at the school."

Think positively. "Life is about problem solving and conflict resolution. I want to read anything that paints a picture of moxie, drive, determination, and courage; those are compelling, and tells me how someone problem-solves."

23

Our Single Best Piece of Writing Advice

Now that you understand what admissions officers are looking for, how can you demonstrate who you are in approximately 500 words? Before you start writing, ask yourself this question: *"What do I want colleges to know about me that they can't find out from the rest of my application package?"*

That is our single best piece of writing advice, and it comes from talking to admissions officers. We did not make it up from thin air. The question may not seem like such a big deal. But your answer is crucial. Admissions officers know a lot about you. Your application includes all sorts of information about your classes, grades, scores, activities, and other aspects of your student life. But those are just pieces of data. They don't tell the whole story.

In your essays, particularly in a personal statement, you have the chance to reflect on your life. You're only 16 or 17; you may not have had much practice delving deeply into your life. Instead, you've been taught to focus on the future, thinking about education, career, travel, and dreams.

Many of our students tell us they cannot answer that question. They don't know what they want colleges to know about them. We assure them that they can, and we teach them how to reflect. Without an answer, you will have trouble writing a college essay that will help admissions officers decide if you are a good fit for their school.

Answer the Big Question

First, get a little help from someone who knows you well, like a parent, a friend, a trusted teacher, or other adult. Ask what he or she thinks of you. What are your best attributes? Are you industrious? Funny? A leader? Shy? Outgoing? Curious? Are you a risk taker?

Think **characteristics**, not accomplishments. Consider what colleges already know from your application. They know your grades, test scores, awards, clubs, jobs, and the names of your brothers and sisters. They will know if your mom is Canadian or if your sister is an alumnus.

Once you know which characteristic(s) you want to share, look at the prompt (or prompts), and find a story that illustrates the trait you want to share, and answers the prompt.

Well-meaning adults, books and websites will tell you, "Start with an anecdote," or "Show your passion," or "Don't write about sports." That type of advice is not going to help you. A college essay can take many forms. Sample essays, websites full of gimmicks and lists of topics that "got students in" can't take the place of a multi-draft writing process and a focus on you.

Remember – you are interesting. You are worth knowing. Show admissions officers who you really are, in your own voice and your own words.

Would you like to learn more? Check out wowwritingworkshop.com for great resources. Parents, sign up for one of their free parent chats, where they answer your questions so you can guide your child through the essay writing process.

Remember to visit Coach Dan's website www.collegeandbeyondllc.com and Coach Ryan's website www.collegeaidformiddleclass.com

College Applications & Financial Aid Forms

"Practice doesn't make perfect. Perfect practice makes perfect."
— Vince Lombardi, Football Coach

College Application

Over the years, one thing we have learned is that the college admissions process is evolving, with new tools and new ways for students to apply to college every year. While change is never ending and the applications, programs, and tools you will be using to apply to college continue to evolve, below are some *general rules and guidelines* you should follow no matter what type of college application you will be using.

- Think of your application as a personal resume to tell your story and to emphasize what makes you unique.
- You can use the personal statement, interview, essay, audition, transcript, video, portfolio, and letters of recommendation to frame your application to help tell your story.
- Organize and rank your high school activities, extra-curricular activities, and the awards you have received from most impressive to least impressive.
- Consider the amount of time you have put into every activity, the leadership roles you have taken on, and any recognition or achievement you have received along the way.
- This ranking could change from college to college, depending on what you would like to highlight.
- Answer every question. NEVER leave anything blank.
- Look for typos and mistakes.
- Read and follow the directions carefully.
- Not paying close attention to even the smallest details can cause you to have mistakes, inconsistencies, and glaring errors. Inattentiveness and carelessness lead to rejections.

24

Warning: If the essay asks for 500 words, don't write an essay with 501. Colleges give you a word count for a reason, and this is not the time to test them. Many times an admissions representative will run a word count if they believe an essay is over the word limit. Depending on the school and the person reading your essay, this could result in an immediate rejection. Don't gamble your acceptance by not following directions.

We all know the saying, "you only get one chance to make a good first impression", so do everything you can to submit a clean, polished, authentic college application.

Types of College Applications

Let's take a minute to talk about each of the types of college applications that a student might end up filling out.

- **College Specific Application:** Many colleges still administer and process their own college application. In this modern age, colleges have put their applications on-line so that it is easy to complete and submit them. However, some still allow a printed copy to be submitted BUT realize this just slows down the process.

- **The Common Application:** (also called the Common App or CA): With this centralized application, students can apply to near 700 colleges and universities around the world. Students enter in factual demographic information, extracurricular activities, and their current curriculum and grades and complete an essay, picking from 1 of 5 prompts (max 650 words). In addition, many schools have supplemental items for students to complete. The CA goes live Aug 1st.

- **Universal College Application (UCA):** Like the Common App, students have a centralized application that currently allows them to apply to 44 colleges and universities. However, unlike the CA, some colleges do not require an essay or letters of recommendation. The UCA goes live July 1st.

- **The Coalition Application:** This application, created by the *Coalition for Access, Affordability, and Success*, is made up of over 90 member colleges and is a single, centralized platform of online tools to assist students in positioning themselves for these colleges. Each student has a "locker" they can share with counselors, teachers, and mentors, and use in the future to submit their applications. The Coalition institutions say they are committed to broadening access and increasing the affordability of higher education for students from all backgrounds. Students and their families have access to free support from Admissions and Financial Aid personnel at individual institutions. The Coalition website states, "We want you to have the confidence that once admitted to any Coalition school, you can afford to attend."

- **Apply Texas College Application:** Apply Texas was created through a collaborative effort between the Texas Higher Education Coordinating Board and the colleges and 61 universities represented on the site. The goal of the project is to offer a centralized means for both Texas and non-Texas students to apply to the many outstanding postsecondary institutions available in Texas. Do your homework to understand essay and application requirements.

- **<u>University of California College Application</u>:** Used by all 9 of the University of California Universities for admissions by California and Non-California applicants. Do your homework to understand essay and application requirments.

College Admissions

The college admissions and application process provides colleges the ability to review your credentials and determine which applicants are most desirable. Also, it is an opportunity for schools to manage enrollment, meet goals, and improve levels of selectivity. To help colleges with these objectives, they use Early Decision (ED), Early Action (EA), and a Wait List to improve their yields and lower their admit ratio.

Theoretically, colleges know that Early Decision (ED) and Early Action (EA) applicants are more likely to enroll than Regular Decision applicants. If a college can receive more ED applicants, this will improve their overall "yield percentage" and lower their admit ratio.

> Believing that the college admission process is fair is a huge myth. Because you have the right numbers, does not guarantee your acceptance. Follow our advice and develop a good college list and in the end, you will be successful.
> – *Coach Ryan*

One big motivator for colleges to use these types of admission decisions is it leads to a higher overall ranking in magazines (Like US News and World Reports) and other college guidebooks.

24

Early Decision (ED): Colleges have used ED to improve their admission statistics, and it can give a student a considerable advantage when it comes to their admission chances. However, be very careful when applying ED because it is BINDING. If you are completing an ED application, you are indicating a commitment to that school. ED application deadlines occur well in advance of Regular Decision application deadlines: typically between October 15th to December 1st. The college's decision is usually 30 to 45 days after these deadlines. There are some colleges that also offer a second ED deadline as well. ED applicants are admitted, denied, or deferred. If you are deferred, your application is reviewed again with the Regular Decision applications. If you are admitted to your Early Decision College, you are required to withdraw all other college applications. *Remember*: DO NOT submit more than one ED application.

Warning! Only use ED if a university is the student's number one choice AND you can pay the full cost of college at that particular school. Consider getting an early estimate of your financial obligation BEFORE you apply by using the Net Price Calculator on each college's website.

Warning! Make sure you read the ED Acceptance Letter thoroughly. If final acceptance is contingent upon completing your senior year of high school at or above your current GPA level, then DO NOT let your academics "slack off." If you do, you are gambling with your final admittance to your chosen college. Finish strong!

Early Action (EA): Early Action is a non-binding early application. EA is a way for a student to apply early and be notified of a decision by the college earlier in the year. Just like with ED, EA application deadlines occur well in advance of Regular Decision application deadlines: typically between October 15th and December 1st. The College's decision is usually 30 to 45 days after the deadline. Many colleges now offer a second EA deadline as well.

Restrictive Early Action/Single Choice Early Action: This admissions application RESTRICTS a student by NOT allowing a student to apply (EA) or Early Decision (ED) to any other colleges, thus preventing them from applying to multiple colleges. Make sure you read the rules regarding EA before you submit your application. Stanford University, for example, does this with their EA application.

Regular Decision: This is the admissions process used by most students to apply to college. If you do apply ED or EA, make sure you are also submitting Regular Decision applications, just in case your early applications are unsuccessful.

Rolling Admission: Some institutions use rolling admission programs in which the schools will make the admission decision on the applications as soon as they arrive. The admission committee will continue to make these decisions until their freshman class is full.

Wait List: If you happen to be Wait Listed, do not give up. In fact, it means you might still be able to attend the college IF there is room for you. At many of the schools, colleges use the wait list to help manage their admit ratio and yield rates. Colleges know that they have an excellent chance of attracting students to attend their school from the wait list due to their selectivity.

Postponement: If a college accepts you but would like you to wait a semester or even an entire year before enrolling, they will give you a postponement. Some reasons for this might include the college believing a student is not emotionally ready to handle college because of their young age or due to concerns about a recent traumatic event in the student's life. Also, schools will suggest students start the second semester or the next year because the students have lower GPA and test scores. These students' GPA and test scores don't have to be reported to US News & World Report, which keeps them from negatively impacting the college's ranking.

Deferring Enrollment: The student decides to delay his/her enrollment for one or more years while preserving their acceptance status. Students sometimes defer enrollment due to a need to earn and save money or for religious, personal, study abroad, travel or other reasons. If you are considering deferring enrollment, please check with each college early in the admissions process to make sure they allow you to do it. Not all schools do.

Appealing The Rejection: If you happen to receive a Rejection Letter, and you wish to contest or appeal the decision, you must do so immediately after receiving the rejection. Make sure you review all the information you provided the college and look for any mistakes and correct them. If you have taken the SAT/ACT again and scored higher, make sure you update your application and send in the new scores. If allowed, submit additional letters of recommendation. You should also consider having your essay reviewed by a professional (counselor, English teacher, etc.). Also, try to set up an on-campus interview to express your desire to attend the college and practice for the interview beforehand to leave a favorable impression on the individuals who will read your appeal. Finally, re-submit your application. Pleasant persistence is the key to a successful appeal.

Completion of college applications and financial aid forms can be a tag team sport. Students should do both but with their hectic schedules parents often help especially with the financial aid forms. It's OK for mom or dad to review college applications but DO NOT over edit the finished product! *– Coach Dan*

24

Financial Aid Overview

First, let's list a few of the key Financial Aid terms.

Expected Family Contribution (EFC): This is the minimum dollar amount the federal government and the colleges determine that a family must pay at any college. It is used to determine need-based financial aid eligibility. (Refer to Chapter 16.)

Colleges and universities use the Federal Methodology (FM) and/or the Institutional Methodology (IM) to calculate your EFC amount. Your EFC amount can be different because the FM and IM Methodology use slightly different formulas to determine your EFC amount.

Federal Methodology (FM): A need analysis formula used by the federal government to determine your Expected Family Contribution (EFC). The FM can consider the family size, the age of older parent, parent and student assets, taxable and nontaxable income, taxes paid, the number of students attending undergraduate level, and student's dependency status. You will be required to complete the Free Application for Federal Student Aid (FAFSA).

Institutional Methodology (IM): Many private colleges and some public schools require you to complete the CSS Financial Aid Profile (CSS Profile) form in addition to the FAFSA. This process is called the Institutional Methodology (IM) to determine your awarded financial aid. The CSS Profile form will ask more detailed and extensive questions compared to the FAFSA. The IM can consider family size, the age of the older parent, parent and student assets, taxable and nontaxable income, taxes paid, home equity, farm value, the number of students attending undergraduate level, and student's dependency status.

Cost of Attendance (COA): This is the total cost of attending a college. Tuition, fees, room and board, lab fees, personal expenses, travel, and miscellaneous expenses.

Financial Need (FN): Take the Cost of Attendance (COA) and subtract your Expected Family Contribution (EFC). The resulting amount is your financial need (FN) according to the Department of Education and is the maximum amount of Need-based financial aid a student or family is eligible to receive. (Again refer to Chapter 16.)

Need-based Financial Aid Formula:

$$COA - EFC = FN$$

COA – EFC = Need – Resources = Modified Need

Example:

• COA:		$26,000
• EFC:	-	$18,000
• Need:	=	$ 8,000
• Resources (Private scholarship)	-	$ 2,000
• Modified Need	=	$ 6,000

If your EFC is less than the COA, your child may be eligible for need-based financial aid. This can include grants, scholarships, loans, and work-study.

Warning! The actual cost of college and Financial Need (FN) results can vary significantly from the need-based financial aid formula. Some colleges will meet 100% of your FN while other schools will only meet 30% of your FN. The question is what aid are they going to give you to fill this gap? Will it be free money (scholarships and grants) or debt/earned money (loans and work-study)?

If your EFC is more than the COA, your child will receive no need-based financial aid. However, you still have the opportunity to reduce the cost of college with tuition discounts, grants, and other scholarships.

<u>**Scholarships and Grants**</u>: Free Money or money that does not need to be repaid.

<u>**Tuition Discounts/Waivers**</u>: Tuition fee reduction or a discount given to students. This is free money that does not need to be paid back.

<u>**Loans**</u>: Money you have to pay back. Loans are offered to students and parents by the Federal Government (most advantageous) and private lenders.

24

<u>Federal Work Study</u>: Jobs that are on or off campus to help students pay for college. These are usually minimum-wage jobs, and many different opportunities exist on campus on a first-come, first-served basis, so do not delay looking for jobs on campus IF you are notified you are eligible for this opportunity.

<u>Scholarships:</u> Awarded based on merit or need. Scholarships can be awarded by state public schools, as well as private institutions. In general, scholarships are awarded based on merit: where students meet qualifying numbers for standardized test scores and GPA. Some scholarships have a "financial need" component that needs to be met to be eligible. Most scholarships are renewable for up to four years and are typically based on meeting minimum GPA requirements while in college. Some scholarships are also based on completing additional community service hours.

<u>Private Scholarship</u>: Awarded from for-profit organizations (e.g., businesses) and non-profit organizations (e.g., churches, foundations, and other institutions).

Warning! Schools can penalize students who receive a private scholarship by lowering their financial aid offers, dollar for dollar, once the college is notified that a student has received a private scholarship. Unfortunately, some colleges reduce scholarships and grants FIRST instead of loans and workstudy.

Financial Aid Forms:

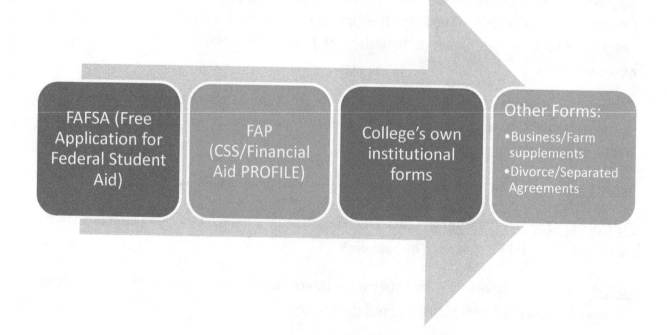

In many cases, State and Institutional Financial Aid is awarded on a first-come, first-served basis. To qualify for any financial aid (need or merit), you will need to complete the required financial aid forms for each college. The important thing is to stay organized and DO NOT miss any deadlines!

Applying for College Financial Aid

To apply for need-based financial aid, you will need to begin by completing the FAFSA (Free Application for Federal Student Aid) and/or the CSS Profile form. Some colleges might also have you complete their own institutional form as well.

All colleges that award federal student aid require students to complete the FAFSA. This form is used to determine a student's eligibility for federal aid, and it is often used for State specific aid as well.

There are approximately 252 colleges that require a family to also complete the CSS Profile. These schools use this detailed financial information to evaluate a student's eligibility for the school's institutional aid, need-based grants, and scholarships. This specific formula is referred to as the Institutional Methodology (IM) of calculating your Expected Family Contribution (EFC). The majority of colleges and universities that require the "Profile" form are selective private schools. However, some flagship state schools such as Georgia Institute of Technology, the University of North Carolina at Chapel Hill, and the University of Michigan at Ann Arbor also require this form in addition to the FAFSA.

24

There is a subgroup of colleges called the "568 Presidents' Group" who use the CSS Profile BUT treat students' assets and the parents' home equity more favorably. They refer to their method of calculating your EFC as the "consensus" methodology.

568 Presidents' Group Member Institutions

Amherst College
Boston College
Claremont McKenna College
College of the Holy Cross
Columbia University
Cornell University
Dartmouth College
Davidson College
Duke University
Georgetown University
Grinnell College
Haverford College

Massachusetts Institute of Technology
Middlebury College
Northwestern University
Pomona College
St. John's College
Swarthmore College
University of Notre Dame
University of Pennsylvania
Vanderbilt University
Wellesley College
Williams College

REMEMBER, while there are two primary forms that need to be completed (FAFSA and CSS Profile); there are actually three methodologies (federal, institutional, and consensus) for calculating a family's Expected Family Contribution (EFC).

Prior – Prior Year (PPY) Filing Format

In October 2016, the Prior-Prior Year (PPY) filing format will begin a new era for reporting income on your FAFSA. Under the new rules, the family's aid eligibility "base year" will now be established off of income from two years before a student enrolls in college, as opposed to just one year before.

This change was made to streamline the financial aid process for families and colleges. It will also hopefully help families receive their financial aid award letter much earlier to help them calculate how much it will cost to attend a particular school.

The federal government and colleges will begin to look at your income on your tax return two years before the financial aid is awarded to your student. Below is a chart to help you understand what income tax year the college will be using:

- If your child enters college in 2016, you will use 2015 income tax return.
- If your child enters college in 2017, you will use 2015 income as well.
- If your child enters college in 2018, you will use 2016 income tax return.
- If your child enters college in 2019, you will use 2017 income tax return.

In 2017-2018, the CSS Profile will also be using the PPY tax information as the basis for calculating the family's need.

Continue on to Chapter 25 and take action today!

Remember to visit Coach Dan's website www.collegeandbeyondllc.com
and Coach Ryan's website www.collegeaidformiddleclass.com
if you need help and to find additional resources!

Print a Copy of Your College Applications and insert them into your College Organizer Here:

24

The Student Aid Report (SAR)

"Champions keep playing until they get it right!"   - Billie Jean King, Tennis Player

The Student Aid Report (SAR) is a government-type report that summarizes the information that you provided on the FAFSA financial aid form. The following are some guidelines involving the SAR.

Your SAR will usually contain your Expected Family Contribution (EFC), the number used to determine your eligibility for federal student aid. Your EFC will appear in the upper right-hand corner of a paper SAR and at (or near) the top of an electronic SAR. If there is an asterisk positioned next to the EFC figure on the SAR, then the data you submitted has been selected for verification (audit). If you do not have an EFC number on your SAR, then more information may be needed from you to process your data.

If you provided an e-mail address when you applied for aid, you will receive your SAR by e-mail 3-5 days after your FAFSA has been processed. This e-mail will contain a secure link so you can access your SAR online. If you did not provide an e-mail address when you applied for aid, then you will receive a paper SAR by mail in 7-10 days after your FAFSA has been processed. Regardless of whether you applied online, or by paper, your financial data will automatically be sent electronically to the colleges you listed on the FAFSA.

Once you receive the SAR, review it carefully to make sure it's accurate and complete. The school(s) you've selected to receive your SAR will use this information to determine if you're eligible for federal, and possibly non-federal, financial aid.

If you need to make corrections to your SAR, you can make them online using your (the student's) FSA ID. Go to http://www.fafsa.ed.gov and select "Make Correction."

If you received a paper SAR, make any necessary corrections on that SAR and mail it to:

Federal Student Aid Programs
PO Box 4038
Washington, DC 52243-4038

If you do not receive your SAR, call the federal processor at **1-800-4-FED-AID FREE.**

Once your SAR is accurate and complete, the colleges to which you have applied will use this information to determine the amount and type of Federal Financial Aid you will receive. This information may also be used by each college to determine State and Institutional Aid as well. You will receive an Award Letter listing the costs (i.e., tuition, fees, room, board, books, transportation, and miscellaneous expenses) associated with your college(s) and a breakdown of how each school thinks you should pay for college (i.e., scholarships, grants, work-study, and loans).

25

> Even If you qualify for aid, it is up to each individual college to determine if you actually receive any aid and how much they give you.
> – *Coach Ryan*

> Check and double check your numbers! Better to find a mistake now than to pay the price later.
> – *Coach Dan*

Remember to visit Coach Dan's website www.collegeandbeyondllc.com and Coach Ryan's website www.collegeaidformiddleclass.com to find additional resources on this important topic!

Place Your SAR Report Here

Financial Aid Awards, Evaluations & Appeals

"Nothing great was ever achieved without enthusiasm."   - Bobby Knight, Coach

Once the Federal Government (Department of Education) calculates your family's Expected Family Contribution (EFC), it will then be displayed on your Student Aid Report (SAR). And as soon as the colleges receive their copies of your SAR, they may decide to do a verification (audit) of the financial information provided by your family. **Verification** is a simple process for families IF you have submitted your Tax Return. If your financial aid application is selected for verification, the school will require you to submit additional documentation (either electronically or sometimes by mail), such as signed copies of your IRS tax returns, W-2, and 1099 forms. The federal government selects on average 30% of the FAFSAs for verification. However, some public and private colleges will select as many as 100% of the FAFSAs for verification.

The easiest way to take care of verification is to use the IRS Data Retrieval Tool (DRT). Three to five weeks after your tax return has been electronically submitted, you can go back into the FAFSA to make a correction. On the page listing the Parents "Financial Information", a DRT button will appear allowing you to access your tax return. By clicking a couple of buttons, you will be sent out to the IRS website and can download your official income and tax numbers into the FAFSA. Then by hitting submit, you will have completed the verification process.

The Financial Aid Award Letter

After submitting the FAFSA and/or CSS Profile, Award Letters are sent out to all students from the colleges in which they have applied. There will be a delay, obviously, in receiving these Award Letters if a family is selected for verification, so do not delay in processing your tax return and using the DRT option.

26

Every family should compare the financial aid package they receive from each of their colleges. Do not look just at the total amount of aid, but conduct a bottom-line analysis of the net out-of-pocket cost of attending each school. Different schools, for example, have different costs for room and board and also will give out their Institutional Financial Aid in different ways.

After reviewing your Award Letter and depending on the type of college (private vs. public), you may decide to appeal your financial aid package. While private schools have the ability to discount their tuition rates to attract quality students, state public schools are often limited in what they can do to reduce their cost, except through merit and need-based scholarships and grants. Unfortunately, even private college financial aid packages can fall short of what you anticipate. You may also receive an award from one of your second-choice safety schools that is more generous than the offer from your first-choice school. But a school's first financial aid offer does not have to be its last. Improving your aid award is possible.

Appealing an Award

If you are appealing an award package, you must be able to demonstrate that there is a legitimate need for additional aid. For example, maybe someone in your family has had an adverse change in employment, or an unusual family circumstance occurred since the financial aid application was initially completed (e.g., medical issue, disability of a parent, divorce, child support dropped, social security survivor benefits for a child stopped). Since May 1st is the last date to notify colleges of your final decision, you will need to take some swift action.

Three Things You Must Do

As financial aid offers start rolling in (via the school's website, postage, or email), you must do the following IF you want to try for an improved aid package:

1. **Understand the Components** — You have to grasp fully what each school is offering you. Although, financial aid Award Letters vary in format from school to school, they should all contain the following items:

   - Your Cost of Attendance (COA)
   - Your Expected Family Contribution (EFC)
   - Your family's need, if any (COA – EFC = NEED)
   - A listing of each aid source and dollar amount
   - A date by which you must return or accept the Award Letter
   - Information on how to "appeal" in the Award Letter

2. **Compare Packages** — Next, compare your aid packages carefully. They can be as different as night and day. Consider the amount you have to pay out of your pocket now and how much you'll eventually have to repay in the future. In other words, be wary of how much of the award is in the form of loans. Confirm that scholarships and grants are guaranteed each year IF you meet the college's scholarship renewal requirements. **NOTE:** Some schools stick it to students in the 2nd year by reducing free money (e.g., scholarships or grants) even though the student met the requirements.

3. **Respond to the Award Letter** — **DO NOT** delay in responding to this Award Letter just because you are still waiting to hear from other schools. If you don't reply on time, the aid package can be revoked. Responding to an Award Letter does not commit you to attending the school(s); it merely safeguards your award. In responding, you have three choices: you can accept the award in its entirety, you can accept some components and reject others, or you can reject the offer entirely and request a revision in the composition of the package.

If you decide to ask for additional aid, you will need to contact the Financial Aid Administrator (FAA) of the college. Be sure to communicate with the FAA as early as possible because the school's extra discretionary aid runs out fast. Present your case in a well-thought-out and diplomatic manner. If you have a legitimate argument, you will need to support it with documentation.

Time is of the essence, and an improper appeal of your financial award could cost you thousands of dollars so DO NOT DELAY!

If you need help developing an appeal strategy BEFORE discussing it with the Financial Aid Administrator at your future college: contact Coach Dan at www.collegeandbeyondllc.com or Coach Ryan at www.collegeaidformiddleclass.com

Evaluating Your Final College Options

26

10 Items You Should Research Before Ever Committing To A College

Before a student makes a commitment to any college, here are ten other critical areas to consider:

1. The number of course requirements

Course requirements vary widely from school to school. You do not want to find yourself stuck in General Education Classes or Electives (Especially if you took AP, IB or Dual Enrollment classes in high school.) or that do not interest you versus taking the core classes that do.

2. The flexibility of course requirements

Schools that require specific courses can put you in a bind if you would rather take more advanced courses, or if you need to take more remedial courses, to fulfill certain requirements. Be sure to check and confirm that the college allows a choice of course levels to satisfy the various requirements. Also please keep in mind that many top professors at large research universities avoid teaching required courses (e.g., Biology 101 or Chemistry 101) filled with hundreds of students. Instead, these courses are often taught by Teachers Assistants (TA's).

3. The availability of your college major

Do your homework and never assume your college of choice offers every possible major, especially if you have a very specialized major in mind. It's critical to check the list of majors at each college BEFORE you decide to go there. At certain colleges, some majors are not open to all students, especially majors for a talent or skill (e.g., music or art), or those that are extremely popular or tough to get into (e.g., engineering or nursing).

4. The availability of your desired classes

In the past few years; college enrollments have risen, but the faculty size has not grown commensurately. As a result, there may be very long wait lists for some classes and shortages in first-year classes for students who did not register on the first possible orientation scheduling date. Be sure to check the availability of your desired courses before sending in your acceptance letter to the college.

5. The availability of professors teaching the course

At many state universities, a significant number of instructors are graduate students. It's important to know how much of your instruction, especially in the first years of college, will be handed over to graduate student teachers. It's okay if a regular professor gives the lectures and the grad student leads discussion or review sessions; however, you may feel slighted if the entire course is ultimately taught by a grad students.

6. The student/faculty ratio

If you attend a school with 10 to 20 students per faculty member, you're likely to get a lot of individual attention from the Instructors. Once the number of students per faculty member goes above 20 or 30, you may not get much, if any, hand-holding from a professor.

7. The percentage of students who graduate

The idea of graduating from college in 4 years can be compromised when students change their majors, end up retaking a class to improve their grade or transfer schools. For this reason, many colleges list their 5 and 6 year graduation rates which are often more impressive than their 4 year rates. A college with a 6 year graduation rate over 80 percent is really good, and a graduation rate of 50 to 70 percent is quite normal; however, there are some colleges and universities whose graduation rate is under 50 percent. Do your homework and check out the average time it takes a student to earn their degree from each of your selected colleges. It is a good idea to avoid schools whose students take an average of 6 to 7 years to graduate. You can go to www.collegedata.com to find this detailed information out about various colleges. Remember, some degrees do indeed take more than 4 years to complete (e.g., Engineering, Physical Therapy, and Medicine).

8. The quality of the career placement department

Very few students even think to ask about the career placement department at the colleges they are considering, but this should be a key item on your checklist assuming the student would like to graduate and find a job. Students should ask questions such as, "What job placement services are provided by the placement office?" What percentage of graduates are employed prior to graduation?", and "Which companies and organizations recruit the schools graduates?"

9. Are you required to take computer–taught or online classes?

To save money, some colleges use virtual online course instruction or have their lectures posted online, rather than use live instructors. It's the new do-it-yourself method of instruction, which may not be the best learning experience for your student.

26

10. The total cost of college

If you plan to attend college, then you should know up front what the total cost of college will be to get a degree. The student should research any opportunities to receive financial aid to help offset that total cost. You will need to find the answers to questions such as:

- ☐ How does the college financially reward a good student?
- ☐ What forms are used by the college to determine financial aid eligibility?
- ☐ What percentage of students, who are eligible to receive financial aid, are actually awarded it and on average how much do they receive?

- ☐ What non-need based or merit based grants and scholarships are available from the college and on average how much do students receive?
- ☐ What is the average debt incurred by each student upon graduation?

To get this important information, students need to do their research. Check out the college guides and the college websites. Ask admissions officers, financial aid officers, students, and recent graduates of the schools. Send e-mails to the appropriate college contacts.

Regardless of how you get this information, it is crucial to make your best possible college choice and get the most out of your college experience. Make it a point to visit websites like www.collegeboard.com and www.collegedata.com to gain valuable insight into each of your colleges. BEFORE you pick your final college, clearly understand these ten important items about each of them and choose wisely!

Finish strong and move on to Chapter 27!

Don't forget to inform the colleges of any special circumstances that you were not able to highlight on the financial aid forms - medical bills, grandparents living with you, loss of job, etc... Aid administrators may lower your EFC number based on your circumstances.
– *Coach Ryan*

The day of reckoning comes when the final Financial Aid Award Letters roll in from each of your colleges. Check to make sure they reflect what you were expecting and if not, call the financial aid office ASAP. Also, do your homework to make sure next year's award is going to look the same. There is nothing worse than getting a nasty surprise in year two of college with a reduced aid package! Believe me, it can happen! – *Coach Dan*

College Admissions Terms

We hope you find this list of words and definitions to be helpful as you navigate your way through every aspect of the college admissions process.

Acceptance Letter - Official letter sent from the admissions department notifying the student s/he has been accepted and admitted to the college.

Accommodations - Services offered to students with Disabilities who take the ACT, SAT or PSAT and are given one of more of the following: extended time, computer use for essays, extra and extended breaks, reading and seeing accommodations, four function calculator, and the ability to bring snacks.

Advanced Placement Program® (AP®) - 35 college level courses offered and administered by the College Board and taught at many high schools. Students often have the opportunity to earn college credit, depending upon the colleges they apply to in the future based on the score they earn (1 to 5) on the final exams in May.

AP Scholar - Recognition given by the College Board to students who have taken 3 or more full-year AP courses and have scored a 3 or higher on final AP exams.

AP Scholar with Honor - Recognition given to students who have taken 4 or more AP exams on full-year courses and have received a 3.25 on all AP exams taken.

AP Scholar with Distinction - Recognition given to students who have taken 5 or more AP Exams on full-year courses and have received an average grade of 3.5 on all AP exams taken.

American College Test (ACT®) - A Standardized Test used by most colleges as part of their admissions review.

27

Associate of Arts Degree (AA) - A two-year degree given by community colleges or other junior colleges to a student who has completed all of their required studies.

Bachelor's Degree or baccalaureate degree (e.g., Bachelor of Arts (BA), Bachelor of Science (BS)) - A college degree given by an undergraduate college or university to a student who has completed all of their required studies, usually in four years.

Branch Campus - A smaller regional campus of a larger university where a student can start for 2 years and then apply to matriculate into and finish up his/her degree at the main campus.

Class Rank - How a student's GPA compares to other students in his/her high school.

Coalition Application – A college application, created by the *Coalition for Access, Affordability and Success*, is made up of over 90 member colleges and is a single platform of online tools to assist students in positioning themselves for these colleges.

College Board - Organization responsible for processing the CSS Profile Financial Aid Form and administering the PSAT, SAT, AP and SAT Subject Test exams.

College Fair - A formal event sponsored by high schools or the NACAC (National Association of College Admission Counseling) where admissions representatives from public and private colleges and universities hand out information about their institutions and answer questions.

College Interview - A formal or informal meeting conducted by an alumnus or college official that allows the college representative to ask questions of the student to verify his/her qualifications and which gives a student the ability to ask questions about the college or university.

College List - A list of 6 to 10 colleges that fit a student's academic, financial, social and geographical wants and needs.

College Prep Courses - High School courses offered to students who meet the recommended or required subjects for college admissions.

College Representative (college rep) – Individuals who serve as the face of the colleges and universities out in the field and are responsible for traveling to designated parts of the country or even internationally to help recruit students to their schools by visiting high schools and doing college fairs. At admissions time, these individuals are the first reviewers of student applications from their assigned areas.

College Rankings – A list comparing colleges based on a set matrix of selection criteria. Publications that try to rank colleges from across the country most notable include Forbes, Princeton Review, US News & World Report, and Washington Monthly.

College Scholarship Service Profile (CSS Profile®) - A financial aid application processed by the College Board for a select group of colleges. This form requests more in-depth financial information from the student and parents for a college to review (in addition to the FAFSA) and is used to determine how much, if any, institutional financial aid a student will receive in their final aid package.

Common Application (Common App) - An online or hardcopy application accepted by over 500+ colleges and universities in the US and at some overseas institutions. Some of these schools also require students to complete supplemental information (e.g., essays, additional questions).

Community College - Two-year colleges (sometimes called junior colleges) that provide affordable postsecondary education as a pathway to an associate's degree or a four-year degree.

Consortium Colleges – Colleges that have shared use of educational and cultural resources and facilities, including a joint automated library system, open cross-registration, and open theater auditions; Joint departments and programs; Inter-campus transportation.

Co-operative Program (Co-op) - Job Training opportunities available at some colleges to students in particular majors, where they are partnered up with local, regional, national and international employers.

Core Curriculum - Courses students are required to take and pass in college in order to graduate.

Cost of Attendance (COA) - The total amount it will cost a student to attend a college: tuition, fees, room, board, books, transportation and miscellaneous expenses.

College Credits – recognition given a student for college courses completed. Students are usually awarded credit for classes based on the Carnegie unit that defines a semester unit of credit as being equal to a minimum of 3 hours of work per week for a semester, trimester, or quarter. However, some courses receive less credit.

Default – Failure to make a timely payment on a college loan. Not paying a loan on time comes with penalties and severe consequences so never take out more in college loans than you can afford to repay based on your future career path. Choose wisely!

Deferral - A notification from the Admissions Department informing a student that his/her Early Action (EA) or Early Decision (ED) admission has been postponed UNTIL after the regular admissions application process is completed.

27

Deferred Admission - An offer to a student allowing him/her to delay enrollment until the Winter or Spring Term instead of the Fall Term at their chosen college.

Demonstrated interest - The process a student needs to go through to show his/her sincere interest in a particular college. Some of the easiest ways to show interest in a college include: officially visiting the campus, attending local college fairs, meeting with Admissions Representatives, staying in contact with these Reps, and signing up for email updates and college newsletters.

Demonstrated Need - The amount of money still needed by a student to pay for college after taking the Cost of Attendance (COA) of a college and subtracting the Expected Family Contribution (EFC).

Denial Letter - A formal letter from an applied for college letting a student know s/he has not been admitted.

Dual Enrollment – A college level course taken by a high school student where s/he has the ability to earn college credit. In some cases, classes are offered at his/her high school and in other cases, students must go to a college to take these classes. **CAUTION:** Confirm which option your future college expects to honor the college credit earned.

Early Action (EA) – A non-binding college application program that allows a student to apply to a college in October or November and receive a final admissions decision by December.

Early Action Single Choice (Restricted Early Action) – A non-binding early admissions option that restricts students from applying to other colleges early action, early notification or early decision. Applicants must sign a statement with their parents confirming s/he will not apply this way to any other college. Stanford University is an example of a school that uses Restricted Early Action.

Early Decision (ED) – A binding college application program which allows students to apply by the first or fifteenth of November and where students usually receive an admissions decision by the middle of December. Since this is binding, students who are accepted are obligated to attend the college UNLESS financial circumstances make it impossible.

Early Decision II (EDII) - A few colleges offer a 2nd round of binding Early Decision in January with admissions decisions (admitted, denied or deferred) sent out usually within six weeks.

Educational Opportunity Program (EOP) - An admissions program offered by many colleges to disadvantaged, underrepresented, first-generation, minority college students where they receive financial aid and academic support services.

Elective - A college course taken by a student that is NOT required for graduation.

Expected Family Contribution (EFC) - The minimum dollar amount a family is expected to pay for the first year of college, determined after submitting the FAFSA and/or CSS Profile.

Extracurricular Activities - Anything done in addition to regular courses taken including community service or volunteer work, talent (art, music, etc.), sports, hobbies, a small business, or clubs.

Fair Test (The National Center for Fair and Open Testing) – A non-profit organization which helps to advance quality education and equal opportunity in colleges, promoting those colleges who have opted to go "Test Optional", accepting students without an ACT or SAT.

Federal Direct (Stafford) Loan – Low-interest rate loan issued by the Federal Government available to undergraduate and graduate students to help pay for college with a maximum loan amount that varies by grade level. These loans are offered to students without a credit score, job or co-signer and must be repaid over time.

Federal Work-study Program - Part-time jobs offered to students on a college campus based on financial need and often listed on the Financial Aid Award Letter.

Fee Waiver – An official decision by a college to waive the application fees for students who are experiencing significant financial challenges or are on free-and-reduced lunch at their high school.

Financial Aid Award Letter - A letter detailing how each college thinks a student and his/her parents should be able to pay for the colleges COA and may include grants, scholarships, loans and possibly work-study opportunities.

Free Application for Federal Student Aid (FAFSA) - The financial aid form families must complete online (or sometimes in paper form) to apply for Federal, State and College financial aid that includes: grants, loans, work-study and some scholarships.

Gap Year - A year taken off between finishing high school and starting college. No college classes of any kind can be taken during this time IF a student is hoping to qualify for future college scholarships as an incoming freshman.

General Education (Gen Ed) - College courses a student must take as part of their overall college curriculum to meet graduation requirements.

27

General Education Development (GED) Certificate – A certificate (in place of a high school diploma) which certifies a person has met the high school level skills based on passing five subject tests.

Grade Point Average (GPA) – The average of a student's individual high school course grades. Many colleges will recalculate a student's GPA because across the country and even within the same state, school districts might use different GPA scales (e.g., Unweighted, Honors, and Weighted). However the standard unweighted scale is usually on a four-point scale: A = 4, B = 3, C = 2, D = 1, F = 0.

Grant – A sum of free money given to a student by a college, the federal or state government, or a private or non-profit corporation or foundation to be used to help pay for college.

Graduate Student - A student who continues to study at a university for a post-undergraduate degree such as a Master's Degree or Ph.D.

Greek system - The system of fraternities and sororities located on or around a college campus. If going "Greek" is important to you, make sure you do your research to confirm your future college offers fraternities and sororities on their campus.

Guidance Counselor, High School Counselor, College Counselor, College Adviser - High School faculty members whose responsibilities might include helping students with class scheduling, setting academic goals, career guidance, college admissions, and social advice, just to name a few.

Honors Classes - Advanced high school courses offered to students (often prior to or in conjunction with them taking Advanced Placement classes).

Honors Program or Honors College – A selected group of students who often live in an honors dorm, attend smaller honors classes; have customized courses, enriched individualized learning, research opportunities and mentoring. Getting admitted to an Honors Program or College is a great way to take the BIG out of a large university while gaining all of the benefits of everything the school has to offer.

Humanities - Courses offered in religion, philosophy, literature, foreign languages, and art.

Independent - A status given to a student when s/he turns age 24 as of Jan 1st of the academic year, is a college graduate and begins a Masters Degree or Medical/Dental School program, is married, has a child, a veteran of the US Armed Forces, is an orphan, homeless or ward of the court.

Independent Educational Consultant or Counselor – Private counselor hired by parents to help their son or daughter and family navigate their way through every aspect of the college process.

International Student - A student who is not a permanent resident of the United States and does not have a US passport or green card.

International Baccalaureate (IB®) – Courses offered to high school students where s/he can earn college credit at many colleges and universities (similar to Advanced Placement courses).

Ivy League Colleges (The Ivies) - 8 colleges located in the United States where admissions is highly selective, including Brown, Columbia, Cornell, Dartmouth, Harvard, the University of Pennsylvania, Princeton, and Yale.

Legacy – Applying to a college where your parent, grandparent, aunt, uncle or sibling is an alumnus which may give an admissions advantage. **Caution**: some colleges, like Duke, proudly boast that they do not favor Legacy applicants.

Learning Disability (LD) - A difference in how a student sees, hears, and understands things. Some of the most common skills s/he may struggle with are spelling, reading, listening, writing, reasoning, speaking and/or math. Check to make sure future colleges have strong LD services and resources on campus.

Letters of Recommendation – A letter written on behalf of a student from teachers, counselors, coaches, pastors, employers or other interested parties. These letters are sometimes required and in other cases optional for college admissions and scholarship consideration.

Liberal Arts - College courses that include the arts, foreign language, humanities, mathematics and natural science.

Liberal Arts College – A College or University that focuses on the liberal arts as a whole or as part of its core curriculum or major offering.

Loan – The amount of money a student or parent borrows with interest from a lender.

Loan Consolidation – Combining all student college student loans into a single loan with one payment. Parents also have the ability combine their PLUS Loans. It is usually easy to consolidate Federal Loans but may not be as easy with private loans, especially if there are multiple lenders.

27

MBA (Master of Business Administration) – A master's degree programs is often pursued by students who are working toward leadership and management positions at their current or future employer. This is a 1 to 3 year degree program offered on campus and also online by some colleges.

Major – An academic area of concentration chosen by a student either when s/he enters college (ex. Engineering) or that (often) must be declared at the start of their junior year.

Masters Degree – A degree program some students pursue in a specific subject area after completing his/her undergraduate degree that takes 1 to 3 years to complete. In some careers, a master's degree is expected to be completed and, in others, it is optional but has the potential to lead to future increased earnings and leadership roles.

Merit Awards, Merit-Based Scholarships – Grants and scholarships awarded NOT based on financial need but instead on performance (or merit) in specific areas (e.g., academics, athletics, artistic talent, or other unique fields).

Minor - An area of study requiring fewer credits, either directly related to or secondary to a student's primary major concentration (for example, Computer Informatics major with a minor in Cybersecurity).

National AP Scholar - Recognition given to students in the United States who score an average of 4 or more on all the Advanced Placement (AP) exams they have taken.

National Merit Scholarship – A scholarship program students may qualify for in their junior year based on their PSAT/NMSQT scores. Nearly 34,000 students receive Letters of Commendation, 16,000 qualify as Semi-finalists, and 15,000 then go on to be Finalists. About 8,000 students are chosen to become Merit Scholarship winners.

Need-based Financial Aid – Aid that is dependent upon a student's and parents' financial situation. Based on income and asset values, a student might be able to qualify for need-based scholarships, grants, loans and work-study.

Need-blind admission – An admissions decision made by a college on whether to admit or deny a student, WITHOUT taking into consideration whether or not that student has a financial need. The vast majority of colleges are need blind when it comes to making final admissions decisions.

Open admission – Admitting any student with a high school diploma. This practice is a very common with community colleges in the United States.

Pell Grant Program – A federally backed program that provides need-based grant money to undergraduate students who have a significant financial need when it comes to paying for college.

PLUS Loan (Parent Loan for Undergraduate Student) – A federal loan program for parents to help a dependent student pay for college. Independent Graduate students can also take out a Graduate PLUS Loan after they have exhausted all available subsidized and unsubsidized Direct Stafford Loans.

PreACT – A test administered in the 10th grade that includes shorter versions of the ACT: English, Math, Reading, and Science sections, but it will not include the optional essay section. It will provide "predictive scores" on the ACT's familiar 1-36 score scale.

Preferred Packaging – A practice in the financial aid department where the most desirable students get the very best financial aid package for a school.

Preliminary SAT (PSAT)/NMSQT® – A test administered by the College Board to juniors in October which acts as a practice for the SAT® and SAT Subject Tests and is used to qualify students for the National Merit Scholarship.

Prerequisites – Those critical items a student MUST complete in order to meet the requirements for future courses.

Principal – The base amount of money borrowed or the portion of that base amount that still needs to be paid back, in addition to any interest charged on top of the principal amount of the loan.

Prior – Prior Year (PPY) - Starting in October 2016, the Prior-Prior Year (PPY) filing format will begin a new era for reporting income on your FAFSA. Under the new rules, the family's aid eligibility "base year" will now be established off of income from two years before a student enrolls in college, versus one year.

Private Loans – College loans a student or parents can take out on their own, outside of the college federal loan program from private lenders to help pay for college. These types of loans often require a student to obtain a co-signer and also can be difficult to consolidate in the future, especially if from multiple lenders.

Quarter system – A system used by some colleges where the academic year is split up into four regular terms and a summer quarter as well. Some colleges also throw in a winter option.

Rejection letter – A letter sent by a college to a student informing him/her that s/he has not been accepted for admissions.

27

Reserve Officers' Training Corps (ROTC) – Offered at many colleges, this program combines military education classes with regular Bachelors Degree classes. In order for students to receive the extra financial aid offered to students in the ROTC program, they must commit themselves to future service in the Air Force, Army, Marines or Navy. Please note that a minimum military obligation after college is a part of the contract.

Residency Requirements – The length of time a family must live in a state in order for the student to qualify for "in-state" tuition rates.

Resident Adviser – An upper-class student, graduate or adult who lives in a dormitory to monitor, support, and advise the dorm residents.

Rolling Admissions – An admissions process where the college considers applications and the supporting documents (transcripts, test scores, etc.) as they are received. Rolling Admissions decisions are often made in short order, and admissions decisions are sent out promptly.

SAT® - A college admissions entrance test offered seven times a year in the United States and six times overseas. Like the ACT, it is used by many colleges as part of the admissions process.

SAT Subject Tests ™ - Specific topic tests offered by the College Board covering 20 topics and divided into 5 categories: English, history, languages, mathematics, and science.

Selective Service – All males are required to register with the Selective Service System (the military draft) to qualify for financial aid.

Semester System - An academic year divided into two equal terms, usually 18 weeks each. There may also be a shorter summer term as well.

Services for Students with Disabilities (SSD) – Assistance provided by the ACT and College Board to students with physical and mental disabilities or challenges where they may receive modifications so that they can take these tests. Disabilities may include Attention Deficit Disorder, certain diseases, and conditions such as diabetes, deafness or hard-of-hearing problems, learning disabilities, physical handicaps, and blindness or vision problems.

Student Aid Report (SAR) - A form generated after you submit your FAFSA that is either emailed or mailed to you, detailing all the information you provided on your FAFSA (assuming no changes needed to be made) and confirming your Expected Family Contribution (EFC) which is then used by the colleges to determine your Financial Aid Package.

Subsidized Loan – A Federal Student Loan offered to some students on the basis of financial need where interest is paid by the government while the student is in college, and for up to 6 months after graduation.

Teaching Assistant (TA) – A graduate student who helps a professor by teaching a portion of a large undergraduate course at a college or university.

Term – A certain period of time (term of the loan) by which every college loan is expected to be paid off.

Test of English as a Foreign Language (TOEFL) – An English test colleges often require International students to take as part of the admissions process at the school. Many colleges have a minimum score which a student must achieve.

Transcript - The official record of a student's courses completed and grades received in high school.

Trimester - An academic year in college, divided into three terms of about three months each, including a summer session.

Tuition - The amount colleges and universities charge for academic instruction on a quarterly, semester or trimester basis.

Tuition Tax Credits – A credit (given by the IRS) to a family on their tax return which helps to reduce their overall tax bill on a dollar-for-dollar basis IF they qualify for the tuition tax credit. Consult your CPA.

Undergraduate: A college student who is earning a bachelor's degree at 4-year College or university.

Universal College Application – A standard admissions application accepted by some colleges.

Unsubsidized Loan - A Federal Student Loan offered to all students where interest is charged from the date the loan is taken out.

Unweighted GPA – The GPA given to students in regular courses taken in high school usually based on a 1 to 4 point range.

Waitlist - A list of applicants whom a college did not accept in the first round of admissions who still may get a chance to get admitted IF there are still spaces available AFTER admitted students make their final decisions.

Weighted GPA – A higher point value GPA given to students in more challenging courses (such as Honors, AP or IB), and factored into a student's cumulative GPA.

Yield Rate - The percentage of accepted applicants who enroll in a college compared to the number of acceptances offered.

27

Remember to visit Coach Dan's website www.collegeandbeyondllc.com
and Coach Ryan's website www.collegeaidformiddleclass.com
if you need help and to find additional resources!

College Contacts, Booklets and Mail

This chapter is one of the most important sections in this binder to help you stay organized during the college process.

Over your high school years, you will receive an incredible amount of marketing materials, mail and emails, from colleges doing everything they can to convince you they are the right college for you; big state schools, and everywhere in between. You will continue to receive this type of correspondence until the end of your senior year so having a place to store everything you want to keep from the colleges you are actually interested in is important. We suggest you get rid of (recycle) all marketing materials from schools that do not interest you. **Do not let this paperwork pile up! Take action today and get organized. Let's get started.**

Your first step is to list the college name at the top of the page. Next write your username and password for the college's website. You will be asked to create a username and password for each college to which you apply and having this information handy will be very important in the future.

Take the time to list the names, phone numbers, e-mail address, etc. of anyone you have contacted (and those who have contacted you or you have met in person) at each college. Knowing who to contact with future questions will make your life easier and you never know having a connection with these individuals personally could help at college admissions selection time too! Remember, colleges have many different departments, and they are usually run independently. For example, if you contact the Financial Aid Department asking about freshman scholarships, they may send you instead to the Admissions Department. Make it a point to record this critical information on the corresponding college contact sheet!

Also use this section to place the notes you have taken on each college for future reference. We suggest you insert a **page protector** for each college so you can put any large or awkward booklets you receive in one central location. Letters and other standard correspondence can be put in a **clear sleeve** or 3-hole punched and placed in this section too. You never know when you will need to refer to this information in the future. Moreover, you will be able to flip through what the school is choosing to highlight or market to you as you do your college research and prepare for future interviews.

Having all of this information organized and in one place will make your life much easier!

28

Print off MULTIPLE copies for all of the colleges you decide to apply to in the future!

College Name:

- Website User Name:
- Password:

Contact
- Department:
- Name:
- Tel:
- Email:

Contact
- Department:
- Name:
- Tel:
- Email:

Contact
- Department:
- Name:
- Tel:
- Email:

Contact
- Department:
- Name:
- Tel:
- Email:

Contact
- Department:
- Name:
- Tel:
- Email:

Notes:

_____

_____

_____

_____

_____

_____

_____

_____

_____

_____

_____

_____

_____

_____

28

_____

_____

_____

College Booklets & Mail

 Insert page protectors or clear sleeves to hold college materials.

 Insert college booklets & pamphlets from the colleges to which you are applying in the future.

 Letters and other standard correspondence can be 3-hole punched and placed within this section.

Remember to visit Coach Dan's website www.collegeandbeyondllc.com and Coach Ryan's website www.collegeaidformiddleclass.com if you have additional questions!

About the Authors

As the son of a teacher and a middle-school principal that struggled to pay for their two boys to attend college, as well as having a family with two children of his own, Ryan decided to investigate why attending college had become so expensive. He found out that the old strategies for getting into college and receiving financial assistance for college that he was taught in high school, and that are still perpetuated today, have changed dramatically. Universities have become much more sophisticated, and the admission process has become more competitive and complicated.

Ryan also realized that there are options available to help families with selecting colleges, but those same options did very little to educate these same parents on how to help lower the cost or help these families pay for college. Ryan became extremely dissatisfied with the current state of college planning and decided to fill this education and coaching gap by founding Clark College Funding Inc. in 2004.

As founder and CEO of Clark College Funding Inc., Ryan has extensive experience in working with over a thousand families throughout the United States in helping them through the entire college planning process.

He holds designations from the National Institute of Certified College Planners. He is a member of the National Association of College Advisers (NACA), National College Advocacy Group (NCAG), Higher Education Consultants Association (HECA), Southern Association for College Admission Counseling (SACAC), and the North Carolina School Counselor Association (NCSCA).

In recognition of his outstanding work, Ryan's book, College Aid for Middle-Class America: How to Pay Wholesale vs. Retail, has been endorsed by nationally known CPA and the President and Founder of the National Association of College Planners, Rick Darvis.

Ryan is a recognized college aid expert, consultant, speaker, author, and coach. He is frequently interviewed on the radio, published in newspapers, magazines, and online, including CBS Money Watch, The Business Insider, and MarketEDU.com.

Ryan created a step-by-step college planning system, which produces exceptional and predictable results of paying wholesale college pricing for any student, from any economic background. As an expert in helping families throughout the U.S. reduce the "financial elephant" of paying for college, he has assisted close to a thousand families save an average of $40,000 to $60,000 of college cost per child.

Ryan holds an MBA from Queens University in Charlotte and is an alumnus of the United States Merchant Marine Academy where he earned an ABET accredited Bachelor's Degree in Marine Systems Engineering. He is also a retired Lieutenant in the U.S. Naval Reserve and has a U.S. Coast Guard License as a Third Asst. Engineer (unlimited tonnage). As founder and CEO of Clark College Funding and Tuition Publishing, he has enabled thousands of families to obtain a quality college degree for less than they dreamed possible and he will show you too!

Dan Bisig is an Author, College Admissions, and Funding Expert, and Founder of *College and Beyond, LLC* (2006) and co-founder of *College and Beyond – Test Prep* (2013). For years Dan has talked about writing a book to help every family navigate their way through the college process and co-authoring the *College Entrance Game Plan: Your Comprehensive Guide To Collecting, Organizing and Funding College (2016)* is a dream come true.

Dan started *College and Beyond* when a longtime friend and client came to him asking what he and his wife should do. They had a daughter (junior) at an all girls private high school, a son (freshman) at an all boys private high school and another daughter at a private grade school. The problem was they only had $5,000 saved for college. Never wanting to turn away a challenge, Dan started doing some research and was ultimately able to help this family set up a complete college funding plan. Success was achieved by integrating and coordinating multiple strategies to pay for college. It was during this time that Dan realized there had to be many more families who also needed help working their way through the college process and his college consulting business was born.

Over the years, Dan has helped guide thousands of students and parents across the United States by connecting the dots of the entire college process including: career and college selection, scholarships, comprehensive admissions guidance (applications, essay review, and interview prep), financial aid review, and building an integrated and coordinated college funding plan. Financial Planners, CPA's and other trusted advisers love to refer clients to Dan because he provides value added guidance on the college process while they offer the right funding and tax solutions for their clients.

Dan has been featured in numerous articles on college issues over the years in the *Cincinnati Business Courier, The Cincinnati Enquirer, Cincinnati Magazine, and Florence Recorder.* He has also been interviewed on local TV and radio shows on a variety of college topics. Dan has spoken in front of thousands of families at many private and public high schools, corporations, libraries, and community organizations in the Greater Cincinnati and Northern Kentucky area.

Dan earned a Bachelor's degree from Eastern Kentucky University in 1988 where he studied business and music. He is a member of the Kentucky Association for College Admission Counseling (**KYACAC**), the Higher Education Consultants Association (**HECA**), and the National College Advocacy Group (**NCAG**). Dan also volunteers his time at **Crossroad Church in Florence, KY**, is an instructor for **Dave Ramsey's Financial Peace University,** a member of the intake team at **LifeLine Ministries** and is a Board Member for the **Boone County Education Foundation (BCEF)**.

When Should You Consider Hiring A Private College Counselor?

After reading the **College Entrance Game Plan**, you may be asking yourself, what do we do if we still have questions on part or all of the college process? The answer may be to hire a private college counselor or independent educational consultant to help you.

Some of the reasons to consider reaching out for help from an expert:

1. Your teen is still struggling with identifying what career or major to pursue.
2. Everyone in your family is just too busy to slow down and take action.
3. You still haven't figured out how your family is going to pay for college.
4. Your teen is having a tough time identifying and narrowing down his/her college short list of schools to apply to in the future.
5. The pressure of the college process is creating major conflict and stress in your family.

So how do you find a reputable College Consultant? Here are 10 things to take into consideration when making your selection.

1. They never guarantee admission to a college.
2. They are honest and open about their fees upfront.
3. They offer different types of packages, with affordability in mind.
4. They do not offer to write your essay or complete your application for you.
5. They do not exaggerate their qualifications.
6. They are affiliated with member organizations, such as HECA, IECA, and NACAC.
7. They visit colleges and meet with admissions directors to keep up with the evolving campus culture and academic changes.
8. They attend training workshops and professional conferences.
9. They do not receive compensation in exchange for placement to a particular college.
10. They do not compromise anyone or anything to try to get you into a top school.

Please remember that we, Dan Bisig and Ryan Clark, work with families all across the United States helping them navigate their way through every aspect of the college process. You can contact us at:

Dan Bisig

College and Beyond, LLC
75 Cavalier Boulevard, Suite 321
Florence, KY 41042

(W) 859-283-2655   (C) 513-919-2646

danbisig@collegeandbeyondllc.com

www.collegeandbeyondllc.com

Ryan Clark

Clark College Funding Inc.
10130 Mallard Creek Road, Suite 300
Charlotte, NC 28262

(W) 704-944-3543   (C) 704-996-7017

rclark@clarkcollegefunding.com

www.collegeaidformiddleclass.com